Positioning: The Battle for Your Mind

Other books written by Al Ries and Jack Trout

Marketing Warfare
Bottom Up Marketing
Horse Sense
The 22 Immutable Laws of Marketing

By Al Ries

Focus
*The 22 Immutable Laws of Branding**
*The 11 Immutable Laws of Internet Branding**

By Jack Trout

The New Positioning
The Power of Simplicity
Differentiate or Die

**With Laura Ries*

Positioning: The Battle for Your Mind

Twentieth Anniversary Edition

By
Al Ries, Chairman
Ries & Ries
and
Jack Trout, President
Trout & Partners Ltd.

Mc Graw Hill Education

McGraw Hill Education (India) Private Limited
NEW DELHI

McGraw Hill Education Offices
New Delhi New York St Louis San Francisco Auckland Bogotá Caracas
Kuala Lumpur Lisbon London Madrid Mexico City Milan Montreal
San Juan Santiago Singapore Sydney Tokyo Toronto

McGraw Hill Education (India) Private Limited

21st reprint 2016
RZCCRRLQRAZZC

McGraw Hill Education (India) Edition 2003

Reprinted in India by arrangement with McGraw-Hill Global Education Holdings, LLC, New York

Sales territories: India, Pakistan, Nepal, Bangladesh, Sri Lanka and Bhutan

ISBN-13: 978-0-07-053375-2
ISBN-10: 0-07-053375-X

Published by McGraw Hill Education (India) Private Limited,
P-24, Green Park Extension New Delhi 110 016, and printed at
Adarsh Printers, New Delhi 110 032

Visit us at: www.mheducation.co.in

Dedicated to the second best advertising agency in the whole world.

Whoever they might be.

Positioning became a roaring success, the buzzword of advertising and marketing people around the world.

Yet the success of the concept had the unintended consequences of pushing Trout & Ries out of the advertising business and into the marketing strategy business.

As it turned out, clients didn't want their advertising agencies to be "strategic"; they wanted them to be "creative." The clients would do their own positioning.

So be it. We became marketing strategists and never looked back.

Contents

Positioning: The Battle for Your Mind

Introduction

"What we have here is a failure to communicate."

How often have you heard that bromide? "Failure to communicate" is the single, most common, most universal reason given for problems that develop.

Business problems, government problems, labor problems, marriage problems.

If only people took the time to communicate their feelings, to explain their reasons, the assumption is that many of the problems of the world would somehow disappear. People seem to believe any problem can be solved if only the parties sit down and talk.

Unlikely.

Today, communication itself is the problem. We have become the world's first overcommunicated society. Each year, we send more and receive less.

A New Approach to Communication

This book has been written about a new approach to communication called "positioning." And most of the examples are from the most difficult of all forms of communication.

Advertising. A form of communication that, from the point of view of the recipient, is held in low esteem. For the most part, advertising is unwanted and unliked. In some cases, detested.

To many intellectuals, advertising is selling your soul to corporate America. Not worthy of serious study.

In spite of its reputation, or perhaps because of it, the field of advertising is a superb testing ground for theories of communication. If it works in advertising, most likely it will work in politics, religion or any activity that requires mass communication.

So the examples in this book could just as well have been taken from the field of politics, war, business or even the science of chasing the opposite sex. Or any form of human activity which involves influencing the minds of other people. Whether you want to promote a car, a cola, a computer, a candidate or your own career.

Positioning is a concept that has changed the nature of advertising. A concept so simple people have difficulty understanding how powerful it is.

We got carried away. The "big lie" was never a part of positioning thinking. On the other hand, we got many calls from Washington political strategists for more information about our positioning concepts.

Adolf Hitler practiced positioning. So does Procter & Gamble as well as every successful politician.

Positioning Defined

Positioning starts with a product. A piece of merchandise, a service, a company, an institution, or even a person. Perhaps yourself.

But positioning is not what you do to a product. Positioning is what you do to the mind of the prospect. That is, you position the product in the mind of the prospect.

A newer definition: "How you differentiate yourself in the mind of your prospect."

So it's incorrect to call the concept "product positioning." As if you were doing something to the product itself.

Not that positioning doesn't involve change. It does. But changes made in the name, the price and the package are really not changes in the product at all.

They're basically cosmetic changes done for the purpose of securing a worthwhile position in the prospect's mind.

Positioning is also the first body of thought that comes to grips with the problems of getting heard in our overcommunicated society.

Thanks to the personal interest of Rance Crain, editorial director of *Advertising Age*, the magazine ran a three-part series on "positioning" in its April 24, May 1, and May 8, 1972 issues. More than any other single event, this series made positioning famous. It also made a deep impression in our minds about the power of publicity.

How Positioning Got Started

If one word can be said to have marked the course of advertising in the past decade, the word is "positioning."

Positioning has become the buzzword of advertising and marketing people. Not only in America, but around the world.

Most people think positioning got started in 1972 when we wrote a series of articles entitled "The Positioning Era" for the trade paper *Advertising Age*.

Since then, we have given more than 500 speeches on positioning to advertising groups in 16 different countries around the world. And we have given away more than 120,000 copies of our "little orange booklet" which reprints the *Advertising Age* articles.

Unfortunately, "vagueness" is becoming more prevalent today than "positioning."

Positioning has changed the way the advertising game is being played today.

"We're the third largest-selling coffee in America," say the Sanka radio commercials.

The third largest? Whatever happened to those good old advertising words like "first" and "best" and "finest"?

Well, the good old advertising days are gone forever and so are the words. Today you find comparatives, not superlatives.

"Avis is only No. 2 in rent-a-cars, so why go with us? We try harder."

"Honeywell, the other computer company."

"Seven-Up: the uncola."

Along Madison Avenue, these are called positioning slogans. And the advertising people who write them spend their time and research money looking for positions, or holes, in the marketplace.

But positioning has stirred up interest well beyond Madison Avenue. With good reason.

Anyone can use positioning strategy to get ahead in the game of life. And look at it this way: If you don't understand and use the principles, your competitors undoubtedly will.

The original Avis positioning ad with the most famous last line in advertising history: "The line at our counter is shorter."

1 What Positioning Is All About

How did a hard-sell concept like positioning become so popular in a business noted for its creativity?

In truth, the past decade might well be characterized as a "return to reality." White knights and black eye patches gave way to such positioning concepts as Lite Beer's "Everything you've always wanted in a great beer. And less."

Poetic? Yes. Artful? Yes. But also a straightforward, clearly defined explanation of the basic positioning premise.

To be successful today, you must touch base with reality. And the reality that really counts is what's already in the prospect's mind.

To be creative, to create something that doesn't already exist in the mind, is becoming more and more difficult. If not impossible.

The basic approach of positioning is not to create something new and different. But to manipulate what's already up there in the mind. To retie the connections that already exist.

We had no idea what "too many" really meant. Average supermarket now has 40,000 SKUs or stock keeping units.

Today's marketplace is no longer responsive to the strategies that worked in the past. There are just too many products, too many companies, and too much marketing noise.

The question most frequently asked is why. Why do we need a new approach to advertising and marketing?

The Overcommunicated Society

The $200 per-capita figure was based on a broad definition of advertising. If you count "media expenditures" only, the actual 1972 number was about $110 per person. Today, the comparable number is $880. Truly we live in an over-communicated society and it's not getting any better.

The answer is that we have become an overcommunicated society. The per-capita consumption of advertising in America today is about $200 a year.

If you spend $1 million a year on advertising, you are bombarding the average consumer with less than a half-cent of advertising, spread out over 365 days. A consumer already exposed to $200 worth of advertising from other companies.

In our overcommunicated society, to talk about the impact of your advertising is to seriously overstate the potential effectiveness of your message. It's an egocentric view that bears no relationship to the realities of the marketplace.

In the communication jungle out there, the only hope to score big is to be selective, to concentrate on narrow targets, to practice segmentation. In a word, "positioning."

The mind, as a defense against the volume of today's communications, screens and rejects much of the information offered it. In general, the mind accepts only that which matches prior knowledge or experience.

Millions of dollars have been wasted trying to

change minds with advertising. Once a mind is made up, it's almost impossible to change it. Certainly not with a weak force like advertising. "Don't confuse me with the facts, my mind's made up." That's a way of life for most people.

The average person can tolerate being told something which he or she knows nothing about. (Which is why "news" is an effective advertising approach.) But the average person cannot tolerate being told he or she is wrong. Mind-changing is the road to advertising disaster.

The folly of trying to change a human mind became one of the most important tenets of the positioning concept. This is the one principle most often violated by marketing people. Literally millions of dollars are wasted every day by companies trying to change the minds of their prospects.

The Oversimplified Mind

The only defense a person has in our overcommunicated society is an oversimplified mind.

Not unless they repeal the law of nature that gives us only 24 hours in a day will they find a way to stuff more into the mind.

The average mind is already a dripping sponge that can only soak up more information at the expense of what's already there. Yet we continue to pour more information into that supersaturated sponge and are disappointed when our messages fail to get through.

Advertising, of course, is only the tip of the communication iceberg. We communicate with each other in a wide variety of bewildering ways. And in a geometrically increasing volume.

The medium may not be the message, but it does seriously affect the message. Instead of a transmission system, the medium acts like a filter. Only a tiny frac-

DIRECTV

Satellite television, of course, has become a big deal and most consumers already have their 50 channels to choose from. Today the talk is about 500 channels in the future. We're not too sure about this prediction. Who needs 500 channels when the average consumer watches no more than 5 or 6 channels?

500 channels? By the time you find something to look at, the show will be over.

tion of the original material ends up in the mind of the receiver.

Furthermore, what we receive is influenced by the nature of our overcommunicated society. "Glittering generalities" have become a way of life in our overcommunicated society. Not to mention that they work.

Technically, we are capable of increasing the volume of communication at least tenfold. Already there's talk of direct television broadcasting from satellites. Every home would have 50 channels or so to choose from.

And there's more to come. Texas Instruments has announced a "magnetic bubble" memory device which can store 92,000 bits of information on a single chip. Six times as much as the largest semiconductor memory device now on the market.

Terrific. But who is working on a magnetic bubble for the mind? Who is trying to help the prospect cope with complexity that so overwhelms the mind that the average reaction to the wealth of information today is to tighten the intake valve? To accept less and less of what is so freely available? Communication itself is the communication problem.

The Oversimplified Message

The best approach to take in our overcommunicated society is the oversimplified message.

In communication, as in architecture, less is more. You have to sharpen your message to cut into the mind. You have to jettison the ambiguities, simplify the message, and then simplify it some more if you want to make a long-lasting impression.

People who depend on communication for their livelihood know the necessity of oversimplification.

Let's say you are meeting with a politician whom you are trying to get elected. In the first five minutes, you'll learn more about your political product than the average voter is going to learn in the next five years.

Since so little material about your candidate is ever going to get into the mind of the voter, your job is really not a "communication" project in the ordinary meaning of the word.

It's a selection project. You have to select the material that has the best chance of getting through.

The enemy that is keeping your messages from hitting pay dirt is the volume of communication. Only when you appreciate the nature of the problem can you understand the solution.

When you want to communicate the advantages of a political candidate or a product or even yourself, you must turn things inside out.

You look for the solution to your problem not inside the product, not even inside your own mind.

You look for the solution to your problem inside the prospect's mind.

In other words, since so little of your message is going to get through anyway, you ignore the sending side and concentrate on the receiving end. You concentrate on the perceptions of the prospect. Not the reality of the product.

"In politics," says John Lindsay, "the perception

The positioning concept of the oversimplified message was further developed into our theory of "owning a word in the mind." Volvo owns "safety." BMW owns "driving," FedEx owns "overnight," Crest owns "cavities."

Once you own a word in the mind, you have to use it or lose it.

is the reality." So, too, in advertising, in business and in life.

But what about truth? What about the facts of the situation?

What is truth? What is objective reality? Every human being seems to believe intuitively that he or she alone holds the key to universal truth. When we talk about truth, what truth are we talking about? The view from the inside or the view from the outside?

It does make a difference. In the words of another era, "The customer is always right." And by extension, the seller or communicator is always wrong.

It may be cynical to accept the premise that the sender is wrong and the receiver is right. But you really have no other choice. Not if you want to get your message accepted by another human mind.

Besides, who's to say that the view from the inside looking out is any more accurate than the view from the outside looking in?

By turning the process around, by focusing on the prospect rather than the product, you simplify the selection process. You also learn principles and concepts that can greatly increase your communication effectiveness.

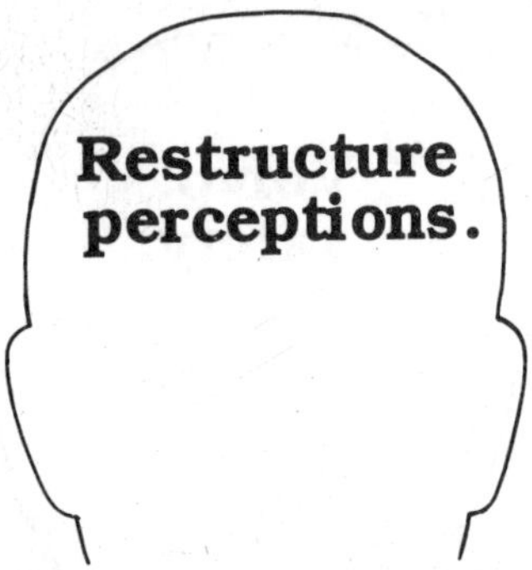

Truth is irrelevant. What matters are the perceptions that exist in the mind. The essence of positioning thinking is to accept the perceptions as reality and then restructure those perceptions to create the position you desire. We later called this process "outside-in" thinking.

The study of psychology is very useful in understanding how minds work. Advertising is "psychology in practice."

2 The Assault on the Mind

As a nation we have fallen in love with the concept of "communication." (In some progressive grade schools even "show and tell" is now being called "communication.") We don't always appreciate the damage being done by our overcommunicated society.

In communication, more is less. Our extravagant use of communication to solve a host of business and social problems has so jammed our channels that only a tiny fraction of all messages actually get through. And not the most important ones either.

One of the remarkable developments in the last 20 years has been the spread of marketing thinking around the world. In many of the developed countries, advertising volume is approaching U.S. levels. Today, America accounts for less than one-third of the world's advertising volume.

The Transmission Traffic Jam

Take advertising, for example. With only 6 percent of the world's population, America consumes 57 percent of the world's advertising. (And you thought our use of energy was extravagant. Actually, we consume only 33 percent of the world's energy.)

Advertising, of course, is only a small channel in the communication river.

It's now 1,000 books a day. The Library of Congress alone adds 300,000 volumes to its collection each year.

Take books. Each year some 30,000 books are published in America. Every year another 30,000. Which doesn't sound like a lot until you realize it would take 17 years of reading 24 hours a day just to finish one year's output.

Who can keep up?

Take newspapers. Each year American newspapers use more than 10 million tons of newsprint. Which means that the average person consumes 94 pounds of newsprint a year. (Roughly the same as their annual consumption of beef.)

There's some question whether the average person can digest all this information. The Sunday edition of a large metropolitan newspaper like *The New York Times* might contain some 500,000 words. To read it all, at an average reading speed of 300 words per minute, would take almost 28 hours. Not only would your Sunday be shot, but also a good part of the rest of the week too.

Internet
Television
Radio
Magazines
Newspaper
Books

Each new medium did not replace an existing medium. Rather, each medium changed and modified all the previous media. Radio used to be an entertainment medium. Today radio is a news, music and talk medium. Houston alone has 185 channels. There are now 12,458 radio stations. There's no sign that this communication assault on the mind is not going to continue far into the future. The average Sunday issue of *The New York Times* still contains some 500,000 words.

How much is getting through?

Take television. A medium barely 30 years old. A powerful and pervasive medium, television didn't replace radio or newspapers or magazines. Each of the three older media is bigger and stronger than it ever was.

Television is an additive medium. And the amount of communication added by television is awesome.

Ninety-eight percent of all American homes have at least one television set. (A third have two or more.)

Ninety-six percent of all television households can

receive four or more TV stations. (A third can receive ten or more.)

The average American family watches television 7 hours and 22 minutes a day. (More than 51 hours a week.)

Like motion pictures, the TV picture is really a still picture which changes 30 times a second. Which means the average American family is exposed to some 795,000 television pictures a day.

Not only are we being pictured to death, we are being formed to death. Take that Xerox machine down the hall. American business currently has more than 324 billion documents on hand. Each year another 72 billion are added to the pile. (Just to print the forms costs more than $4 billion a year.)

Down the halls at the Pentagon, copy machines crank out 350,000 pages a day for distribution throughout the Defense Department. Equal to 1,000 good-sized novels.

"World War II will end," said Field Marshal Montgomery, "when the warring nations run out of paper."

Take packaging. An 8-ounce package of Total breakfast cereal contains 1,268 words of copy on the box. Plus an offer for a free booklet on nutrition. (Which contains another 3,200 words.)

The assault on the mind takes place in many different ways. The U.S. Congress passes some 500 laws a year (that's bad enough), but regulatory agencies promulgate some 10,000 new rules and regulations in the same amount of time.

The Code of Federal Regulations now contains

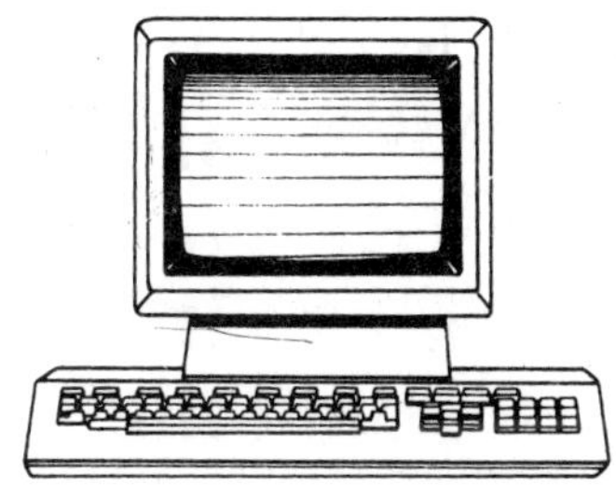

In spite of the rapid adoption of the personal computer by U.S. businesses, we're still drowning in paper. The average office worker uses 250 pounds of copy paper a year. The "paperless office" seems a long way off.

more than 80,000 pages. And is growing by 5,000 pages a year.

At the state level, over 250,000 bills are introduced each year. And 25,000 pass the legislatures to disappear into the labyrinths of the law.

Ignorance of the law is no excuse. Ignorance of the lawmakers apparently is. Our legislators continue to pass thousands of laws that you can't possibly keep track of. And even if you could, you couldn't possibly remember how a law might differ from one state to another.

Who reads, sees or listens to all this outpouring of communication?

There's a traffic jam on the turnpikes of the mind. Engines are overheating. Tempers as well as temperatures are rising.

Brown, Connally and Chevrolet

In 20 years, most people have learned just one more thing about Jerry Brown. He's now mayor of Oakland, California.

How much do you know about Governor Jerry Brown of California?

Most people know just four things. (1) He's young. (2) He's good-looking. (3) He's dated Linda Ronstadt. (4) He's against big government.

Not very much residual effect for the enormous press coverage given a chief executive of the state of California. A man who had four books written about him in a single year.

Aside from the governor of your own state, do you know the names of any of the governors of the other 49 states?

In the 1980 primaries, Big John Connally of Texas

spent $11 million and wound up with one delegate. Whereas virtual unknowns like John Anderson and George Bush wound up with hundreds of delegates.

Connally's problem? He was too well known as a wheeler-dealer. "That perception was so deep," said his campaign strategist, "we couldn't have changed it."

At best, communication in an overcommunicated society is difficult. Yet you are often better off if communication doesn't take place. At least until you are ready to position yourself for the long term. You never get a second chance to make a first impression.

What do the following names mean to you: Camaro, Caprice, Chevette, Concours, Corvette, Impala, Malibu, Monte Carlo, Monza and Vega?

Automobile model names, right? Would you be surprised to learn that these are all Chevrolet models?

Chevrolet is the most heavily advertised product in the world. In a recent year, General Motors spent more than $130 million to promote Chevrolet in the United States. That's $356,000 a day, $15,000 an hour.

What do you know about Chevrolet? About Chevrolet engines, transmissions, tires? About the seats, upholstery, steering?

Be honest. How many Chevrolet models are you familiar with? And do you know the differences between them?

"Baseball, hot dogs, apple pie and Chevrolet." The only answer to the problems of an overcommunicated society is the Chevrolet answer. To cut through the traffic jam in the prospect's mental highway, you must use an oversimplified approach.

Camaro
Cavalier
Corvette
Impala
Lumina
Malibu
Metro
Monte Carlo
Prizm

These nine Chevrolet models for the year 2000 are probably no better known today than the 10 Chevrolet models were in 1972. Because of all this confusion, Chevrolet is now in second place behind Ford.

What this book suggests may seem shocking and immoral to you. (Fortunately, it's not illegal or ineffective.) To cut through the transmission traffic jam, you must use Madison Avenue techniques.

Nearly half the jobs in the United States can be classified as information occupations. Virtually no one is immune from the consequences of a deep involvement in our overcommunicated society.

And virtually everyone can learn to apply the lessons of Madison Avenue to his or her own life. At home and in the office.

No one can predict the future. Add the Internet to the media list. The Internet, in our opinion, will become the greatest of all media with the most impact on our lives.

The Media Explosion

Another reason our messages keep getting lost is the number of media we have invented to serve our communication needs.

There is television. Commercial, cable and pay.

There's radio. AM and FM.

There's outdoor. Posters and billboards.

There are newspapers. Morning, evening, daily, weekly and Sunday.

There are magazines. Mass magazines, class magazines, enthusiast magazines, business magazines, trade magazines.

And, of course, buses, trucks, streetcars, subways and taxicabs. Generally speaking, anything that moves today is carrying a "message from our sponsor."

Today, someone is even trying to put ads on the doors of public bathrooms.

Even the human body has become a walking billboard for Adidas, Gucci, Pucci and Gloria Vanderbilt.

Take advertising again. Just after World War II, the per-capita consumption of advertising in the United States was about $25 a year. Today it's eight times as much. (Inflation accounts for some of this increase, but the volume is also up substantially.)

Do you know eight times as much about the products you buy? You may be exposed to much more advertising, but your mind can't absorb anymore than it used to. There's a finite limit to how much you can take in, and advertising, even at $25 a year, was already way over the limit. That one-quart container that sits on top of your neck can hold just so much.

At $200 per person, the average American consumer is already exposed to twice as much advertising per year as the average Canadian. Four times as much as the average Englishman. And five times as much as the average Frenchman.

While no one doubts the advertiser's financial ability to dish it out, there's some question about the consumer's mental ability to take it all in.

Each day, thousands of advertising messages compete for a share of the prospect's mind. And make no mistake about it, the mind is the battleground. Between 6 inches of gray matter is where the advertising war takes place. And the battle is rough, with no holds barred and no quarter given.

Advertising is a brutal business where mistakes can be costly. But out of the advertising wars, principles have been developed to help you cope with our overcommunicated society.

Product development: 29%
Strategic planning: 27%
Public relations: 16%
Research and development: 14%
Financial strategies: 14%
Advertising: 10%
Legal: 3%

One of the consequences of this rapid increase in advertising volume is the decline in advertising effectiveness and a rise in the use of public relations as a marketing tool. A recent survey of 1,800 executives by the American Advertising Federation about the importance of various functions shows that public relations is more highly regarded than advertising.

The Product Explosion

Another reason our messages keep getting lost is the number of products we have invented to take care of our physical and mental needs.

Take food, for example. The average supermarket in the United States has some 10,000 individual products or brands on display. For the consumer, there's no relief in sight. In fact, the product explosion could get worse. Already in Europe they are building super supermarkets (called hypermarkets) with room for displaying 30,000 to 50,000 products.

The packaged-goods industry obviously expects the proliferation to continue. Those scratch marks on the side of most grocery boxes, the Universal Product Code, represent 10 digits. (Your social security number has only 9. And the system is designed to handle more than 200 million people.)

And this same situation holds in the industrial field. The Thomas Register, for example, lists 80,000 companies. There are 292 manufacturers of centrifugal pumps, 326 builders of electronic controls, to take two categories at random.

There are some 450,000 active trademarks registered at the U.S. Patent Office. And 25,000 new ones get added every year. (Hundreds of thousands of products are sold without trademarks too.)

In a typical year, the 1,500 companies listed on the New York Stock Exchange introduce more than 5,000 "significant" new products. And presumably a lot more than that were insignificant. Not to mention the millions of products and services marketed by America's 4 million other corporations.

Take cigarettes. There are more than 175 brands on the market today. (A vending machine built to hold all these brands might be 30 feet long.)

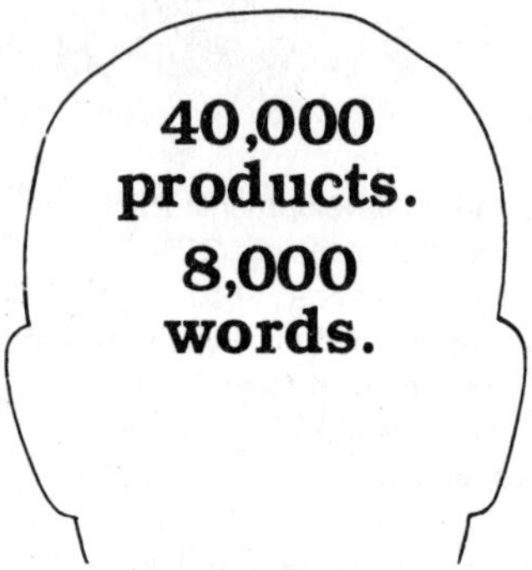

Supermarkets have gotten a lot bigger in just 20 years. The average supermarket now has some 40,000 individual products or brands on display. Compare that with the speaking vocabulary of the average person, which remains at just 8,000 words.

Item	1970s	1990s
Frito Lay chip varieties	10	78
Soft drink brands	20	87
Dental flosses	12	64
Software titles	0	250,000
Running-style shoes	5	285
Contact lens types	1	36
Bottled water brands	16	50
Women's hosiery styles	5	90

Consider these numbers in terms of product explosion.

Take drugs. There are some 100,000 prescription drugs on the U.S. market. While many of these are specialized and used almost exclusively by medical specialists, the general practitioner still has a herculean job to keep informed about the multitude of drug products available.

Herculean? No, it's an impossible job. Even Hercules himself could not have kept up with more than a small fraction of these drugs. To expect more is to be totally ignorant of the finite capacity of even the most brilliant mind.

And how does the average person cope with the product and media explosions? Not very well. Studies on the sensitivity of the human brain have established the existence of a phenomenon called "sensory overload."

Scientists have discovered that a person is capable of receiving only a limited amount of sensation. Beyond a certain point, the brain goes blank and refuses to function normally. (Dentists have been toying with some of these discoveries. Earphones are placed on the patient, and the sound level is turned up until the sensation of pain no longer is felt.)

Thanks to stringent FDA regulations for drug approvals, the number of prescription drugs on the market has not increased very much. Where the real explosion has occurred is in the over-the-counter market. There are now more than 50 varieties of Tylenol.

The Advertising Explosion

Ironically, as the effectiveness of advertising goes down, the use of it goes up. Not just in volume, but in the number of users.

Doctors, lawyers, dentists, accountants are dipping their toes into the advertising pool. Even institutions like churches and government have begun to advertise. (In 1978 the U.S. government spent $128,452,200 on advertising.)

Professional people used to consider advertising beneath their dignity. But even to some professionals, dollars are more important than dignity. So to make a bigger buck, doctors, lawyers, dentists, optometrists, accountants and architects are starting to promote themselves.

Currently there is a raft of legal advertising (Injured? Call 1-800-LAWSUIT) and a raft of advertising by accountants like Arthur Andersen. But Medicare, medicaid, and our tax laws have pretty much driven free enterprise out of the medical profession.

They also face stiffer competition. A decade ago, there were 132,000 lawyers in the United States. Today there are 432,000. Compared with 10 years ago, there are 300,000 more lawyers today beating the bushes for business.

And the same thing is happening in the medical profession. Our overcommunicated society is in the process of becoming an overmedicated one too. According to the Congressional Office of Technology Assessment, by the end of the decade the nation might have 185,000 more physicians than it needs.

How will these excess doctors find patients to practice on? By advertising, of course.

And now we have the dot.com crowd spilling into the media with endless Wall Street money.

But the professionals who are opposed to advertising say it downgrades their profession. And it does. To advertise effectively today, you have to get off your pedestal and put your ear to the ground. You have to get on the same wavelength as the prospect.

In advertising, dignity as well as pride goeth before destruction, and a haughty spirit before a fall.

3 Getting into the Mind

In our overcommunicated society, the paradox is that nothing is more important than communication. With communication going for you, anything is possible. Without it, nothing is possible. No matter how talented and ambitious you may be.

What's called luck is usually an outgrowth of successful communication.

Saying the right things to the right person at the right time. Finding what the NASA people in Houston call a window in space.

Positioning is an organized system for finding windows in the mind. It is based on the concept that communication can only take place at the right time and under the right circumstances.

The Easy Way into the Mind

The easy way to get into a person's mind is to be first. You can demonstrate the validity of this principle by asking yourself a few simple questions.

What's the name of the first person to fly solo across the North Atlantic? Charles Lindbergh, right?

Now, what's the name of the second person to fly solo across the North Atlantic?

Not so easy to answer, is it?

What's the name of the first person to walk on the moon? Neil Armstrong, of course.

What's the name of the second?

What's the name of the highest mountain in the world? Mount Everest in the Himalayas, right?

What's the name of the second highest mountain in the world?

What's the name of the first person you ever made love with?

What do these brands have in common? They were all the first brands in the mind in their categories. Today these brands are still the leading brands in their categories. "It's better to be first than it is to be better" is by far the most powerful positioning idea.

What's the name of the second?

The first person, the first mountain, the first company to occupy the position in the mind is going to be awfully hard to dislodge.

Kodak in photography, IBM in computers, Xerox in plain-paper copiers, Hertz in rent-a-cars, Coca in cola, General in electric.

The first thing you need to "fix your message indelibly in the mind" is not a message at all. It's a mind. An innocent mind. A mind that has not been burnished by someone else's brand.

What's true in business is true in nature too.

"Imprinting" is the term animal biologists use to describe the first encounter between a newborn animal and its natural mother. It takes only a few seconds to fix indelibly in the memory of the young animal the identity of its parent.

You might think all ducks look alike, but even a

day-old duckling will always recognize its mother, no matter how much you mix up the flock.

Well, that's not quite true. If the imprinting process is interrrupted by the substitution of a dog or cat or even a human being, the duckling will treat the substitute as its natural mother. No matter how different the creature looks.

Falling in love is a similar phenomenon. While people are more selective than ducks, they're not nearly as selective as you might think.

What counts most is receptivity. Two people must meet in a situation in which both are receptive to the idea. Both have open windows. That is, neither is deeply in love with someone else.

Marriage, as a human institution, depends on the concept of first being better than best. And so does business.

If you want to be successful in love or in business, you must appreciate the importance of getting into the mind first.

You build brand loyalty in a supermarket the same way you build mate loyalty in a marriage. You get there first and then be careful not give them a reason to switch.

The Hard Way into the Mind

And what if your name is not Charles or Neil or Kleenex or Hertz? What if someone else got into your prospect's mind first?

The hard way to get into a person's mind is second. Second is nowhere.

Bert Hinkler was the second person to fly the Atlantic Ocean solo, but tell the truth, have you ever heard of Bert Hinkler? He left home and his mother hasn't heard from him since. Call home, Bert, your mother is getting worried. (By the way, the second woman to fly the Atlantic Ocean solo was Beryl Markham, another relatively unknown person.)

What's the largest-selling book ever published? (Also the first book ever printed with movable type?) The Bible, of course.

And the second largest-selling book ever published? Who knows?

New York is the largest cargo port in the United States. But which one is second? Would you believe Hampton Roads, Virginia? It's true.

Who was the second person to fly solo across the North Atlantic? (The authors would really like to know the answer to this question. Save your postage: Amelia Earhart was not the second person to fly the North Atlantic solo, although she was the first woman to do it. Now then, who was the second woman?)

If you didn't get into the mind of your prospect first (personally, politically or corporately), then you have a positioning problem.

In a physical contest, the odds favor the fastest horse, the strongest team, the best player. "The race isn't always to the swift, nor the battle to the strong, but that's the way to bet," said Damon Runyan.

Not so in a mental contest. In a mental battle the odds favor the first person, the first product, the first politician to get into the mind of the prospect.

Second can also be successful. Consider those that challenged leaders: Crest vs. Colgate. Fuji vs. Kodak. Avis vs. Hertz. Pepsi vs. Coke. It's No. 3 and No. 4 that have the most serious problems.

In advertising, the first product to establish the position has an enormous advantage. Xerox, Polaroid, Bubble Yum, to name a few more examples.

In advertising, it's best to have the best product in your particular field. But it's even better to be first.

Love might be wonderful the second time around, but nobody cares who the second person to fly solo across the North Atlantic was. Even if that person was a better pilot.

There are positioning strategies to deal with the problem of being number two and number three or even number two hundred and three. (See Chapter 8, "Repositioning the Competition.")

But first make sure you can't find something to be first in.

It's better to be a big fish in a small pond (and then increase the size of the pond) than to be a small fish in a big pond.

Amelia Earhart was the third person to fly the Atlantic Ocean solo, but that's not the reason she got famous. She got famous because she was "first." That is, the first woman to do it. "If you can't be first in a category, then set up a new category you can be first in" is the second most powerful positioning idea.

Advertising Learns the Lesson

The advertising industry learned the Lindbergh lesson the hard way. What the stock market was in the twenties, the advertising business was in the sixties. The go-go sixties, they were called.

While it lasted, the exciting "anything goes" years of the sixties were a marketing orgy.

At the party, it was "everyone into the pool." Little thought was given to failure. With the magic of money and enough bright people, a company felt that any marketing program would succeed.

The wreckage is still washing up on the beach. DuPont's Corfam, Gablinger's beer, the Convair 880, Vote toothpaste, Handy Andy cleaner.

The world will never be the same again, and neither will the advertising business.

As the president of a large consumer products company said recently, "Count on your fingers the number of successful new national brands introduced in the last two years. You won't get to your pinky."

Not that a lot of companies haven't tried. Every supermarket is filled with shelf after shelf of "half successful" brands. The manufacturers of these me-too products cling to the hope that they can develop a brilliant advertising campaign which will lift their offspring into the winner's circle.

Meanwhile, they hang in there with coupons, deals, point-of-purchase displays. But profits are hard to come by, and that "brilliant" advertising campaign, even if it comes, doesn't ever seem to turn the brand around.

No wonder management people turn skeptical when the subject of advertising comes up. And instead of looking for new ways to put the power of advertising to work, management invents schemes for reducing the cost of what they are currently doing. Witness the rise of the house agency, the media buying service, the barter deal.

It's enough to drive an advertising person into the soft ice cream business.

The chaos in the marketplace is a reflection of the fact that advertising just doesn't work the way it used to. But old traditional ways of doing things die hard. "There's no reason why advertising can't do the job," say the defenders of the status quo, "as long as the product is good, the plan is sound and the commercials are creative."

But they overlook one big, loud reason. The marketplace itself. The noise level today is far too high.

Messages prepared in the old, traditional ways have no hope of being successful in today's overcommunicated society.

To understand how we got to where we are today, it might be helpful to take a quick look at recent communication history.

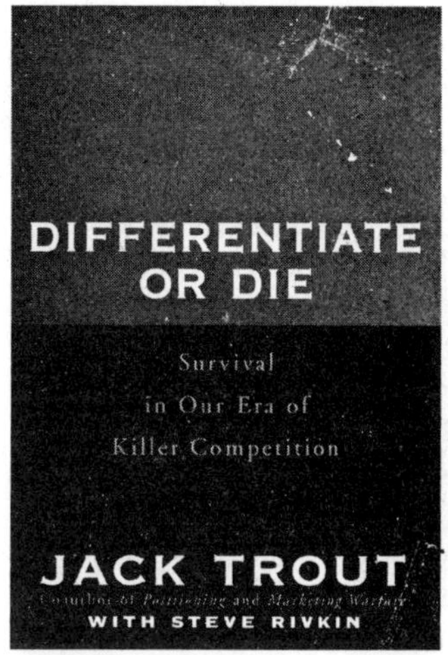

USPs can be established in other ways. See the just published *Differentiate or Die.*

The Product Era

Back in the fifties, advertising was in the product era. In a lot of ways, these were the good old days when the "better mousetrap" and some money to promote it were all you needed.

It was a time when advertising people focused their attention on product features and customer benefits. They looked for, as Rosser Reeves called it, the "Unique Selling Proposition."

But in the late fifties, technology started to rear its ugly head. It became more and more difficult to establish that "USP."

The end of the product era came with an avalanche of me-too products that descended on the market. Your "better mousetrap" was quickly followed by two more just like it. Both claiming to be better than the first one.

Competition was fierce and not always honest. It got so bad that one product manager was overheard to say, "Wouldn't you know it. Last year we had nothing to say, so we put 'new and improved' on the package. This year the research people came up with a real improvement, and we don't know what to say."

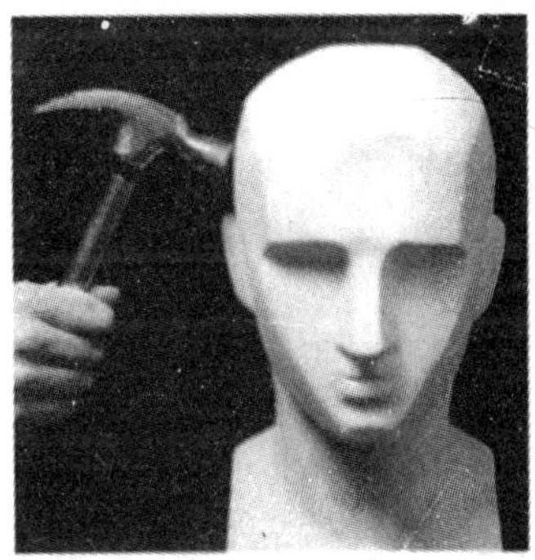

In the fifties, advertising people looked for a unique feature or benefit they could hang their hat on. Then they depended on massive advertising to drive the idea into the mind.

These days, the Federal Trade Commission would severely frown on the "new and improved" language unless the company could prove it.

In the sixties, advertising people found that reputation or image was more important than any single product feature

The Image Era

The next phase was the image era. Successful companies found that reputation, or image, was more important in selling a product than any specific product feature.

The architect of the image era was David Ogilvy. As he said in his famous speech on the subject, "Every advertisement is a long-term investment in the image of a brand." And he proved the validity of his ideas with programs for Hathaway shirts, Rolls-Royce, Schweppes and others.

But just as the me-too products killed the product era, the me-too companies killed the image era. As every company tried to establish a reputation for itself, the noise level became so high that relatively few companies succeeded.

And of the ones that made it, most did it primarily with spectacular technical achievements, not spectacular advertising. Xerox and Polaroid, to name two.

The Positioning Era

Today it has become obvious that advertising is entering a new era. An era where creativity is no longer the key to success.

The fun and games of the sixties and seventies have given way to the harsh realities of the eighties.

To succeed in our overcommunicated society, a company must create a position in the prospect's mind. A position that takes into consideration not only a company's own strengths and weaknesses, but those of its competitors as well.

Advertising is entering an era where strategy is king. In the positioning era, it's not enough to invent or discover something. It may not even be necessary. You must, however, be first to get into the prospect's mind.

IBM didn't invent the computer. Sperry-Rand did. But IBM was the first company to build a computer position in the mind of the prospect.

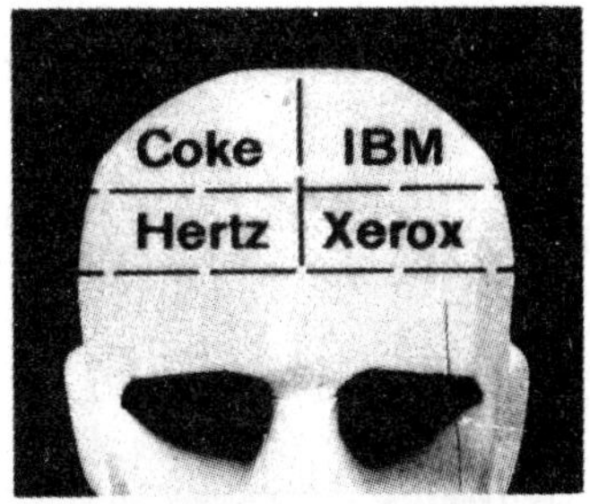

In the seventies, advertising people quickly adopted positioning tactics, which involved the search for a position to occupy in the prospect's mind that was not taken by another brand.

What Amerigo Discovered

The Sperry-Rand of the fifteenth century was Christopher Columbus.

As every schoolchild knows, the man who discovered America was poorly rewarded for his efforts. Christopher Columbus made the mistake of looking for gold and keeping his mouth shut.

Amerigo Vespucci didn't. The IBM of the fifteenth century, Amerigo was five years behind Christopher. But he did two things right.

First, he positioned the New World as a separate continent, totally distinct from Asia. This caused a revolution in the geography of his day.

Second, he wrote extensively of his discoveries and theories. Especially significant are the five letters of his third voyage. One (Mundus Novus) was translated into 40 different languages over a 25-year period.

It didn't take long for the advertising industry to jump on the positioning bandwagon. This ad ran in the United Kingdom a month after the *Ad Age* articles appeared. No credit to us, of course.

Before he died, Spain granted him Castillian citizenship and gave him a major state post.

As a result, the Europeans credited Amerigo Vespucci with the discovery of America and named the place after him.

Christopher Columbus died in jail.

Michelob was not the first high-priced beer to get inside the beer-drinker's mind. Heineken was. So Michelob used the Amelia Earhart strategy. Heineken was the first high-priced *imported* beer, so Michelob became the first high-priced *domestic* beer. Unfortunately, Michelob dropped "First class" for things like "The night belongs to Michelob." Too bad. Michelob could have been one of the two or three best-selling domestic brands of beer.

What Michelob Discovered

The great copywriters of yesterday, who have gone to the big ad agency in the sky, would die all over again if they saw some of the campaigns currently running.

Take beer advertising, for example. In the past a beer copywriter looked closely at the product to find a copy platform. And he or she found product features like "real-draft" Piels and "cold-brewed" Ballantine.

And even further back a beer copywriter searched for just the right words to paint a picture of quality, taste and appetite appeal.

"Just a kiss of the hops."

"From the land of sky blue waters."

"Real gusto in a great light beer."

Today, however, poetry in advertising is as dead as poetry in poetry.

One of the biggest advertising successes of recent times is the campaign for Michelob. The brand was launched with a campaign that is as poetic as a stop sign. And just as effective.

"First class is Michelob" positioned the brand as a premium-priced American-made beer. In only a few years, Michelob has become one of the largest-selling beers in the United States. At premium prices too.

Was Michelob the first premium-priced domestic beer? No, of course not. But Michelob was the first to build the position in the beer-drinker's mind.

What Miller Discovered

Notice how the poetry in that famous Schlitz slogan hides the postioning.

"Real gusto in a great light beer."

Did anyone out there in the neighborhood bar and grill believe that Schlitz was any lighter than Budweiser or Pabst? No, the Schlitz slogan made as much sense to the Billy Carters of this world as the lyrics in an Italian opera.

But over at the Miller Brewing Company, they apparently asked themselves what would happen if they really positioned a beer as a light beer.

So Miller introduced "Lite" beer. And the rest is history. A runaway success that spawned a host of me-too brands. Including, ironically, Schlitz Light. (Presumably to be promoted as: "Real gusto in a great light-light beer.")

For many people or products today, one roadway to success is to look at what your competitors are doing and then subtract the poetry or creativity which has become a barrier to getting the message into the mind. With a purified and simplified message, you can then penetrate the prospect's mind.

For example, there's also an imported beer whose positioning strategy is so crystal-clear that those old-time beer copywriters probably wouldn't even accept it as advertising.

Positioning isn't everything. Lite beer was a brilliant positioning success, but a legal disaster. Miller found that they couldn't legally own the "light" name in the beer category, so the "Lite" name had to be changed to "Miller Lite" to differentiate the brand from the dozens of other light beers on the market. The Lite lesson: Don't give your brand a generic name. Miller then proceeded to muck-up its light brand with other "Lights" such as Genuine Draft Light and Miller Lite Ice. Now Bud Light is in first place.

"America's favorite German beer" has helped Beck's remain a leading brand of imported beer. Unfortunately, Beck's, a German beer, is stuck with an English name while Heineken, a Dutch beer, is blessed with a German name. The name of your brand is just as important as its positioning, maybe even more important.

"You've tasted the German beer that's the most popular in America. Now taste the German beer that's the most popular in Germany." This is how Beck's beer effectively positioned itself against Lowenbrau.

Advertising like this is making Beck's beer popular in America too. Sales keep going up year after year. Lowenbrau, on the other hand, gave up the struggle and became a domestic brand.

And if the oldtimers are confused by today's beer advertising, what would they think of the TWA campaign: "The only widebodies we fly are the ones people prefer most. The 747 and the L-1011." (In other words, no DC 10s.)

A long way in both concept and execution from that classic airline campaign, "Fly the friendly skies of United."

Strange things have been happening in American advertising. It's becoming distinctly unfriendly. And more effective.

4 Those Little Ladders in Your Head

To better understand what your message is up against, let's take a closer look at the ultimate objective of all communication: the human mind.

Like the memory bank of a computer, the mind has a slot or position for each bit of information it has chosen to retain. In operation, the mind is a lot like a computer.

But there is one important difference. A computer has to accept what you put into it. The mind does not. In fact, it's quite the opposite.

As a defense mechanism against the volume of today's communications, the mind rejects information that doesn't "compute." It accepts only that new information which matches its current state of mind. It filters out everything else.

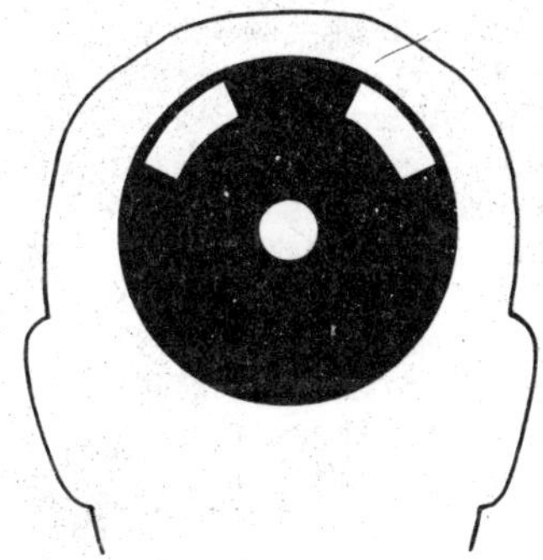

The more we studied the human mind, the more we saw the relationship between the mind and the memory bank of a computer. To put a new brand into the mind, you have to delete or reposition the old brand that already occupies the category. A computer works in exactly the same way.

You See What You Expect to See

Take any two abstract drawings. Write the name Schwartz on one and the name Picasso on the other.

"You taste what you expect to taste." Thirteen years after we wrote those words, Coca-Cola introduced New Coke, a major marketing disaster. Their own research illustrates the folly of trying to "improve" on the taste of the real thing. In blind taste tests, consumers preferred New Coke almost three to one over the original formula. When they were able to see what they were drinking, however, consumers preferred the brand now called Coca-Cola Classic more than four to one.

Then ask someone for an opinion. You see what you expect to see.

Ask two people of opposite persuasion, say, a Democrat and a Republican, to read an article on a controversial subject. Then ask each one if the article changed his or her opinion.

You'll find that the Democrat gets out of the article facts to support one point of view. The Republican gets out of the same article facts to support the opposite point of view. Very little mind changing takes place. You see what you expect to see.

Pour a bottle of Gallo into an empty 50-year-old bottle of French Burgundy. Then carefully decant a glass in front of a friend and ask for an opinion.

You taste what you expect to taste.

Blind taste testings of champagne have often ranked California brands above French ones. With the labels on, this is unlikely to happen.

You taste what you expect to taste.

Were it not so, there would be no role for advertising at all. Were the average consumer rational instead of emotional, there would be no advertising. At least not as we know it today.

One prime objective of all advertising is to heighten expectations. To create the illusion that the product or service will perform the miracles you expect. And presto, it does.

But create the opposite expectation and the product is in trouble. The introductory advertising for Gablinger's beer created a feeling that because it was a diet product, it would taste bad.

And sure enough, the advertising worked! People

tried it and were easily convinced that it did taste bad. You taste what you expect to taste.

An Inadequate Container

Not only does the human mind reject information which does not match its prior knowledge or experience, it doesn't have much prior knowledge or experience to work with.

In our overcommunicated society, the human mind is a totally inadequate container.

According to Harvard psychologist Dr. George A. Miller, the average human mind cannot deal with more than seven units at a time. Which is why seven is a popular number for lists that have to be remembered. Seven-digit phone numbers, the Seven Wonders of the World, seven-card stud, Snow White and the Seven Dwarfs.

"The Magical Number Seven" was the title of Miller's article, which appeared in the March 1956 issue of *The Psychological Review*. In his article, Dr. Miller pointed out a number of famous sevens, including the seven notes of the musical scale and the seven days of the week.

Ask someone to name all the brands he or she remembers in a given product category. Rarely will anyone name more than seven. And that's for a high-interest category. For low-interest products, the average consumer can usually name no more than one or two brands.

Try listing all ten of the Ten Commandments. If that's too difficult, how about the seven danger signals of cancer? Or the four horsemen of the Apocalypse?

Today you have to remember alarm codes, social security, e-mail, fax, calling card and PIN number. Digits are crowding out words.

In one newspaper survey, 80 out of 100 Americans couldn't name a single member of the President's Cabinet. Said a 24-year-old musician, "I don't even think I could name the Vice President "

If our mental storage bowl is too small to handle

questions like these, how in the world are we going to keep track of all those brand names which have been multiplying like rabbits?

Thirty years ago the six leading cigarette companies between them offered the American smoker 17 different brands. Today they sell 176.

There are now over 10 million websites, 250,000 software titles and some 4 million book titles. Each year 77,000 new book titles are added to the pile. (At least this is an old one.)

"Modelitus" has struck every industry, from automobiles to beer to zoom lenses. Detroit currently sells almost 300 different models in a bewildering variety of styles and sizes. Mavericks, Monarchs, Montegos, Monzas. Let's see, is it a Chevrolet Monza or a Mercury Monza? The public is confused.

Simple Saturn, the only automobile brand in America that came in one model only, became very successful. For a number of years, the average Saturn dealer sold more cars than any other dealer. Then what did they do next? You guessed it. They introduced a larger model, the "L" series, "The next big thing from Saturn."

To cope with complexity, people have learned to simplify everything.

When asked to describe an offspring's intellectual progress, a person doesn't usually quote vocabulary statistics, reading comprehension, mathematical ability, etc. "He's in seventh grade" is a typical reply.

People can often remember positioning concepts better than names. A man suffering from brain damage might recognize and refer to his "oldest daughter," even though he might not be able to recall her name.

This ranking of people, objects and brands is not only a convenient method of organizing things, but also an absolute necessity to keep from being overwhelmed by the complexities of life.

The Product Ladder

To cope with the product explosion, people have learned to rank products and brands in the mind. Perhaps this can best be visualized by imagining a series of ladders in the mind. On each step is a brand name. And each different ladder represents a different product category.

Some ladders have many steps. (Seven is many.) Others have few, if any.

A competitor that wants to increase its share of the business must either dislodge the brand above (a task that is usually impossible) or somehow relate its brand to the other company's position.

Yet too many companies embark on marketing and advertising programs as if the competitor's position did not exist. They advertise their products in a vacuum and are disappointed when their messages fail to get through.

Moving up the ladder in the mind can be extremely difficult if the brands above have a strong foothold and no leverage or positioning strategy is applied.

An advertiser who wants to introduce a new product category must carry in a new ladder. This, too, is difficult, especially if the new category is not positioned against the old one. The mind has no room for what's new and different unless it's related to the old.

That's why if you have a truly new product, it's often better to tell the prospect what the product is not, rather than what it is.

The first automobile, for example, was called a "horseless" carriage, a name which allowed the public to position the concept against the existing mode of transportation.

Words like "offtrack" betting, "lead-free" gasoline

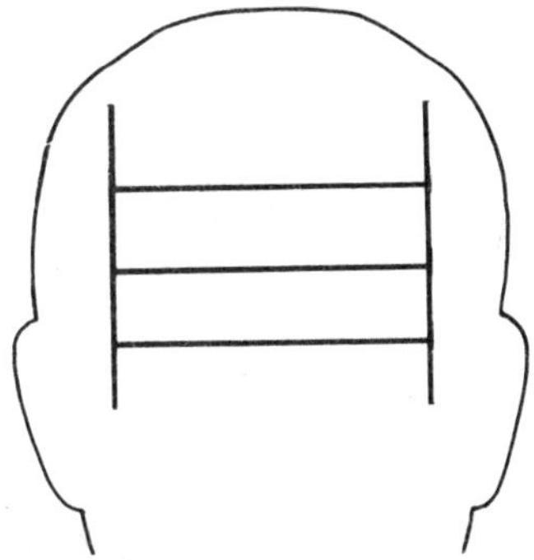

For every product category, a prospect tends to have a ladder like this one in his or her mind with the leader on the top rung, No. 2 on the second rung and No. 3 on the third rung. The number of rungs can vary. Three is the most typical. Seven is probably the maximum. (The rule of seven.)

One category has no rungs on the ladder. (Caskets.) People just don't want to remember any casket names, although there is a leading brand. (Batesville.)

and "tubeless" tire are all examples of how new concepts can best be positioned against the old.

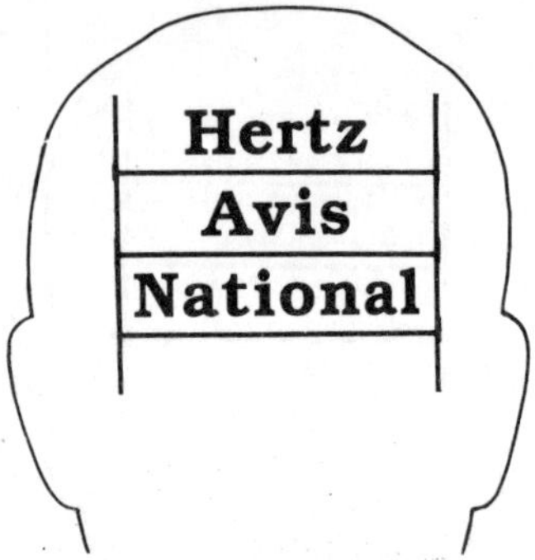

This is the car rental ladder in the typical prospect's mind. Even a customer who rents from Avis or National will generally have this same ladder in his or her mind. People rent from Avis not because the company is on the top rung in their car rental ladder, but in spite of the fact that Avis is not the leader. "Why go with us? We try harder."

Hertz, on the other hand, has made a living by reminding us who is on the top rung. "There's Hertz and there's not exactly."

The "Against" Position

In today's marketplace the competitor's position is just as important as your own. Sometimes more important. An early success in the positioning era was the famous Avis campaign.

The Avis campaign will go down in marketing history as a classic example of establishing the "against" position. In the case of Avis, this was a position against the leader.

"Avis is only No. 2 in rent-a-cars, so why go with us? We try harder."

For 13 years in a row, Avis lost money. Then they admitted that they were No. 2 and Avis started to make money.

The first year Avis made $1.2 million. The second year, $2.6 million. The third year, $5 million. Then the company was sold to ITT.

Avis was able to make substantial gains because they recognized the position of Hertz and didn't try to attack them head-on.

To better understand why the Avis program was so successful, let's look into the mind of the prospect and imagine we can see a product ladder marked "rent-a-cars."

On each rung of the product ladder is a brand name. Hertz on top. Avis on the second rung. National on the third.

Many marketing people have misread the Avis

story. They assume the company was successful because it tried harder.

Not at all. Avis was successful because it related itself to Hertz. (If trying harder were the secret of success, Harold Stassen would have been President many times over.)

Shortly after the positioning book was published, the Federal Trade Commission invited us to Washington, DC to comment on their pending regulation banning the use of "hanging comparisons." According to the proposed regulation, you couldn't say, "We try harder." You would have to say *whom* you tried harder than. We pointed out that the poetry of the Avis slogan resided in the fact that the reader added the thought: "*than Hertz*." The best headline for an advertisement is always incomplete. The best headlines always let the reader supply a word or phrase to complete the idea. That's what makes an advertisement "involving."

As an indication of how far the advertising business has come in its acceptance of comparative ads, *Time* magazine originally rejected the "We try harder" line as being too competitive with Hertz. Other magazines followed the *Time* lead.

So the account executive panicked and agreed to change the line to "We try damned hard." (A curse word presumably being less offensive than a comparative word.)

Only after the ad was canceled did *Time* change its mind and agree to accept the original version. (The account executive was fired.)

Establishing the "against" position is a classic positioning maneuver. If a company isn't the first, then it has to be the first to occupy the No. 2 position. It's not an easy task.

But it can be done. What Avis is doing in rent-a-cars, Burger King is doing in fast foods and Honeywell is doing in computers.

Honeywell has left the computer business. Hewlett-Packard is now No. 2. (But no one knows it, which is an H-P mistake.)

The "Uncola" Position

Another classic positioning strategy is to worm your way onto a ladder owned by someone else. As 7-Up did. The brilliance of this idea can only be appreciated when you comprehend the enormous share of mind

7-Up was fighting a two-front war. The colas were on one front and Sprite was on the other. The uncola campaign was brilliant, but they ultimately lost the battle to Sprite which is now the leading lemon-lime brand. Many things went wrong with 7-Up, including inconsistent advertising, line extension (remember 7-Up Gold?) and a failure to do the obvious thing with the uncola campaign. They told the soft-drink consumer what 7-Up was not. They should have also told the consumer what 7-Up was.

enjoyed by Coke and Pepsi. Almost two out of every three soft drinks consumed in the United States are cola drinks.

By linking the product to what was already in the mind of the prospect, the "uncola" position established 7-Up as an alternative to a cola drink. (The three rungs on the cola ladder might be visualized as: One, Coke. Two, Pepsi. And three, 7-Up.)

With uncola positioning, sales really took off. Since the 1968 uncola unveiling, annual net sales of the Seven-Up Company increased from $87.7 million to over $190 million. Today 7-Up is the world's third largest-selling soft drink.

To prove the universality of positioning concepts, McCormick Communications took beautiful-music radio station WLKW, an also-ran in the Providence (Rhode Island) market, and made it number one. Their theme: WLKW, the unrock station.

To find a unique position, you must ignore conventional logic. Conventional logic says you find your concept inside yourself or inside the product.

Not true. What you must do is look inside the prospect's mind.

You won't find an "uncola" idea inside a 7-Up can. You find it inside the cola drinker's head.

The F.W.M.T.S. Trap

More than anything else, successful positioning requires consistency. You must keep at it year after year.

Yet after a company has executed a brilliant positioning coup, too often it falls into what we call the F.W.M.T.S. trap.

"Forgot what made them successful."

Shortly after the company was sold to ITT, Avis decided it was no longer satisfied with being number two. So it ran ads saying, "Avis is going to be No. 1."

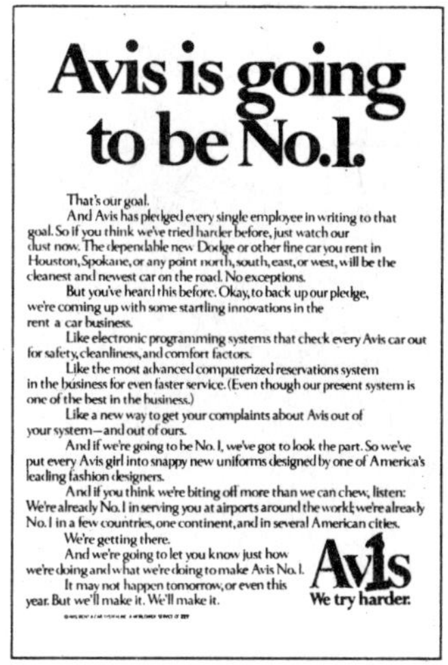

The prospect looks at an advertisement like this and thinks, "No, you're not."

That's advertising your aspirations. Wrong psychologically. And wrong strategically.

Avis was not destined to be No. 1 unless it could find a weakness in Hertz to exploit.

Furthermore, the old campaign not only related No. 2 Avis to No. 1 Hertz on the product ladder in the prospect's mind, but also capitalized on the natural sympathy people have for the underdog.

The new campaign was just conventional brag-and-boast advertising.

Be honest. In the last 20 years, Avis has run many different advertising campaigns. "The wizard of Avis." "You don't have to run through airports."

But what is the single theme that leaps into your mind when someone mentions Avis?

Of course, "Avis is only No. 2, etc." Yet Avis in the last few years has consistently ignored the only concept it really owns in the mind. Someday when National Rent-A-Car passes Avis in sales, Avis will appreciate the value of the No. 2 concept it lost.

If you want to be successful today, you can't ignore the competitor's position. Nor can you walk away from your own. In the immortal words of Joan Didion, "Play it as it lays."

Another advertiser that fell into the F.W.M.T.S.

This advertisement is a typical example of the inconsistent approach used by 7-Up over the years. 7-Up now has half the share of market-leader Sprite. (America was definitely not turning 7-Up.)

trap was 7-Up. With the "uncola" campaign, the company successfully positioned its 7-Up drink as an alternative to Coke and Pepsi. But the current campaign says "America is turning 7-Up."

America is doing no such thing. Seven-Up is also advertising its aspirations. No different conceptually than the "Avis is going to be No. 1" campaign.

And no more effective.

5 You Can't Get There from Here

There's an old story about a traveler who asked a farmer for directions to a nearby town.

The farmer replied, "Well, you go down the road for a mile, turn left at the fork. No, that won't work."

"You turn around and drive for half a mile till you hit a stop sign, then turn right," the farmer continued. "No, that won't work either." After a long pause, the farmer looked at the confused traveler and said, "You know what, son, you can't get there from here!"

That just happens to be the fate of many people, politicians and products today. They happen to be in a position where "they can't get there from here."

America is not turning 7-Up. Avis is not going to be No. 1. Wishing won't make it so. And neither will massive amounts of advertising.

The "Can Do" Spirit Refuses to Die

In many ways our country's Vietnam experience was a typical example of American "can do" spirit. Anything is possible if only you try hard enough. But no matter how hard we tried, no matter how many soldiers and how much money we poured in, the problem could not be solved by an outside force.

We couldn't get there from here.

In spite of hundreds of Vietnam examples to the contrary, we live in a "can do" environment. Yet many things are not possible, no matter how hard you try.

Take the 55-year-old executive vice president who is never going to get the top job. When the chief executive retires in a few years at age 65, the board appoints a 48-year-old successor.

Forget 48-year-olds. Today's high-tech CEOs are in their twenties and thirties.

The 55-year-old is out of phase for the president's job. To have a chance for promotion, he or she must be at least a decade younger than the current holder.

In the battle for the mind, the same thing often happens to the product that's out of phase.

Today a company can have a great product, a great sales force, a great advertising campaign and still fail miserably if it happens to be in a position in which "you can't get there from here." No matter how many millions it is prepared to spend.

And the best example is what happened to RCA in the computer business.

The first article ever written on positioning appeared in the July 1969 issue of *Industrial Marketing* magazine. Even today people ask us, "How does positioning apply to business-to-business products as opposed to consumer ones?" When we tell them that positioning started as an industrial concept, they don't believe us. Why? It doesn't match the perception in the mind that all good advertising ideas start in the consumer area. Lesson: Don't fight perceptions with facts. Perceptions will always win

The Handwriting on the Wall

In 1969 we wrote an article for *Industrial Marketing* magazine using RCA as one of the prime examples. Entitled "Positioning Is a Game People Play in Today's Me-Too Marketplace," the article pulled no punches. It named names and made predictions. All based on the rules of a game called positioning. (It was the first time anyone had used the word "positioning" to describe the process of coping with the mental position that a larger, more established competitor occupies.)

One prediction, in particular, turned out to be strikingly accurate. As far as the computer industry was concerned, we wrote, "A company has no hope to make progress head-on against the position that IBM has established."

The operative word, of course, was "head-on." And while it's possible to compete successfully with a market leader (the article suggested several approaches), the rules of positioning say it can't be done "head-on."

Back in 1969 this raised a few eyebrows. Who were we to say that a powerful, multibillion-dollar company like RCA couldn't find happiness in the computer business if it so desired?

So as 1970 rolled around, it was full speed ahead at RCA. The incredible story was told in the pages of the business press.

"RCA fires a broadside at No. 1," said the headline of an article in the September 19, 1970, issue of *Business Week*.

"RCA goes head-to-head with IBM," said the headline of a news item in the October 1970 issue of *Fortune*.

"RCA computer push is head-on slash at IBM," said the headline of a story in the October 26, 1970, issue of *Advertising Age*.

And just to make sure there was no mistaking the

This is the head-to-head advertisement that RCA ran in *The Wall Street Journal* and other business publications. For many years some people thought that a positioning ad was one that mentioned a competitor in the headline. Not necessarily true. Positioning has nothing to do with whether you mention a competitor or not. It has to do with "considering" competitive strengths and weaknesses before you launch a marketing campaign.

company's intentions, Robert W. Sarnoff, chairman and president, made a prediction that by the end of 1970, RCA would be in a "firm No. 2 position" in the computer industry. Pointing out that his company had already invested "far more to develop a strong position in the computer industry than we have ever put into any previous business venture," including color TV, Mr. Sarnoff said that the goal had been development of a solid profit position in the early seventies.

GE's Jack Welch has all but killed that wishful "can do" stuff. It's one or two or you're out.

The "Can Do" Spirit Dies

Less than a year later, the roof fell in. "The $250 million disaster that hit RCA," said the headline of a story in the September 25, 1971, issue of *Business Week*.

That's a lot of dough. Someone figured out that if you took that much money in one-hundred-dollar bills and put it on the sidewalk in Rockefeller Center, the stack would go right past Bob Sarnoff's window on the 53rd floor of the RCA Building.

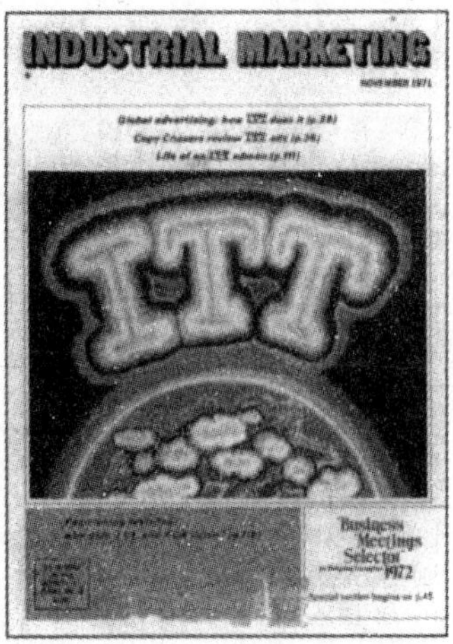

After GE and RCA folded their computer lines, we came back with an article in the November 1971 issue of *Industrial Marketing* magazine. The article lit a fire under the positioning concept and generated many requests for reprints and more information.

Those were bad times for computer manufacturers. In May 1970, after years of unprofitable computer operations, General Electric threw in the sponge by selling the mess to Honeywell.

With two major computer manufacturers folding one right after another, the urge to say "I told you so" was irresistible. So later in the year 1971, we came back with "Positioning Revisited: Why Didn't GE and RCA Listen?" (The article appeared in the November 1971 issue of *Industrial Marketing*.)

How do you advertise and market against a company like IBM? The two positioning articles made some suggestions.

How to Go Against an IBM

The computer business has often been referred to as "Snow White and the Seven Dwarfs." Snow White has established a position unrivaled in the history of marketing.

IBM has 60 percent of the computer business versus less than 10 percent for the largest of the dwarfs.

How do you go against a company with a position like IBM?

Well, first you have to recognize it. Then you don't do the thing that too many people in the computer field try to do. Act like IBM.

A company has no hope to make progress head-on against the position that IBM has established. And history, so far, has proved this to be true.

The small companies in the field probably recognize this. But the big companies seem to think they can take their strong positions against IBM. Well, as one unhappy executive was heard to say, "There just isn't enough money in the world." You can't get there from here.

"Fight fire with fire" is the old cliché. But as the late Howard Gossage used to say, "That's silly. You fight fire with water."

A better strategy for IBM's competitors would be to take advantage of whatever positions they already own in the minds of their prospects and then relate them to

Burroughs
Control Data
GE
Honeywell
NCR
RCA
Univac

These were the seven computer companies unlucky enough to have to compete with IBM in mainframe computers. Which company did the best? None of the above. The winner and ultimately the second largest computer company in the world was Digital Equipment Corp. DEC used the Amelia Earhart approach. They created the minicomputer, a new category they could be first in.

In recent years we've been over at IBM working on the problems of how to replace the concept of "mainframe computers" with an up-to-date position. Our recommendation was to pursue "integrated computing" as their position. Who else can better put all the pieces together?

a new position in computers. For example, how should RCA have positioned its computer line?

Our 1969 article made a suggestion: "RCA is a leader in communications. If they positioned a computer line that related to their business in communications, they could take advantage of their own position. Even though they would be ignoring a great deal of business, they would be establishing a strong beachhead."

Take NCR, a company with a strong position in cash registers.

NCR has made great progress in the computer business by concentrating its efforts on retail data entry systems. Computerized cash registers, if you will.

Where the situation is hopeless, however, the effort in finding a valid position is probably wasted. Much better to concentrate on other areas of a company's business. As Charlie Brown said, "No problem is too big to run away from."

In truth, outright failure is often preferable to mediocre success.

An also-ran can easily be tempted to think that the answer to the problem is trying harder. A company stuck with a losing position is not going to benefit much from hard work.

The problem is not what, but when. The extra effort, if it is going to be of much help, should be applied early to establish the precious posture of product leadership.

With it, everything is possible. Without it, the going is going to be rough indeed. (As the Eskimo

Many companies only get one chance in life. Take the right fork and become enormously successful. Take the wrong fork and wither and die. RCA took the wrong fork and ended up as a secondary brand at General Electric. This is the fork they should have taken. The irony is that communications have become the real growth market for computers of all types. Currently IBM, Sun Microsystems and other computer companies are pouring most of their marketing resources into the battle to dominate the Internet, the ultimate communication network.

NCR succumbed to the siren song and went head to head with IBM. They almost died. Today they are back to "transactions."

remarked, the lead dog is the only one who enjoys a change of view.)

Smith and Jones at General Electric

One example might help illustrate the principle. Two gentlemen had their eyes on the top job at General Electric. One was named Smith. The other was named Jones.

Smith was your typical "can do" corporate executive. So when he was given the computer operation to run, he accepted the assignment with relish.

Jones, on the other hand, was realistic. He knew that GE hadn't gotten into the computer business early enough to dominate it. At this late stage of the game, it was going to cost the company too much to catch up to IBM. If it ever could.

After Smith failed to turn the computer business around, Jones got a chance to participate. He recommended that General Electric get out of the computer business, which it eventually did by selling the operation to Honeywell.

That's one reason why Reginald H. Jones wound up as chief executive of the General Electric Company. And J. Stanford Smith wound up at International Paper.

In a nutshell, the hierarchy in the computer business is duplicated in almost every other industry. Invariably, every industry has a strong leader and a host of also-rans. IBM in computers, Xerox in copiers and General Motors in automobiles.

What we left out of the story was that J. Stanford Smith was the head of the industrial advertising and sales promotion department of General Electric, where both of us started our careers. We knew Stan Smith extremely well. He was perhaps the most brilliant marketing person we have ever known. If Smith couldn't save GE computers, nobody could. This made a deep impression on both of us. You often find yourself in situations where "you can't get there from here."

If one can understand the role of positioning in the computer industry, then one can transfer this knowledge to almost any other situation.

What works for computers will also work for cars and for colas.

Or vice versa.

6 Positioning of a Leader

Companies like Avis and Seven-Up found viable alternative positions to marketing leaders.

But most companies don't want to be an also-ran, successful or not. They want to be a leader like Hertz or Coke.

So how do you get to be the leader? Actually it's quite simple. Remember Charles Lindbergh and Neil Armstrong?

You just get there firstest with the mostest.

Establishing Leadership

History shows that the first brand into the brain, on the average, gets twice the long-term market share of the No. 2 brand and twice again as much as the No. 3 brand. And the relationships are not easily changed.

Look at the intensive marketing battle being fought between Pepsi-Cola and Coca-Cola. In spite of years of successful marketing moves by the Pepsi challenger, who leads the cola race? Why Coca-Cola, of

Campbell's
Carnation
Coca-Cola
Colgate
Crisco
Del Monte
Eveready
Gillette
Gold Medal
Goodyear
Hammermill
Hershey's
Ivory
Kellogg's
Kodak
Life Savers
Lipton
Manhattan
Nabisco
Palmolive
Price Albert
Sherwin-Williams
Singer
Swift
Wrigley's

These are the leading brands in 25 different categories in the year 1923. By the turn of the century, 77 years later, only three brands had lost their leadership. (Eveready, Manhattan, Palmolive.) This is the power of being a leader. Leadership alone is your most effective marketing strategy.

course. For every six bottles of Coke sold, Pepsi manages to sell only four.

Hertz is fine. GM is faltering. Firestone has blown a tire. Westinghouse is gone. It's getting tougher out there.

And so it goes. The leader brand in category after category outsells the number two brand by a wide margin. Hertz outsells Avis, General Motors outsells Ford, Goodyear outsells Firestone, McDonald's outsells Burger King, General Electric outsells Westinghouse.

Many marketing experts overlook the enormous advantages of being first. Too often they attribute successes like Kodak and IBM and Coke to "marketing acumen."

Coca-Cola keeps trying. Currently they are trying to take their PowerAde sports drink against Gatorade. Who will win this battle? Gatorade, of course.

The Failures of Leaders

Yet when the shoe is on the other foot, when a marketing leader isn't first in a new category, the new product is usually an also-ran.

Coca-Cola is a gigantic company compared to Dr. Pepper. Yet when Coke introduced a competitive product, Mr. Pibb, even the immense resources of the Atlanta giant couldn't put much of a dent in Dr. Pepper's sales. Mr. Pibb remains a poor second. For every six bottles of Dr. Pepper sold, Coca-Cola manages to sell only one bottle of Mr. Pibb.

IBM is much bigger than Xerox and has awesome resources of technology, manpower and money. Yet what happened when IBM introduced a line of copiers competitive with Xerox?

Not much. Xerox still has a share of the copier market 10 times that of IBM.

And supposedly Kodak was going to cream Polaroid when the Rochester colossus got into the instant camera business. Far from it. Polaroid's business actually increased while Kodak managed to take only a small share. At the expense of a substantial loss in Kodak's conventional camera business.

Almost all the material advantages accrue to the leader. In the absence of any strong reasons to the contrary, consumers will probably select the same brand for their next purchase as they selected for their last purchase. Stores are more likely to stock the leading brands.

The larger, more successful companies usually have the first pick of outstanding college graduates. In fact, they usually attract more and better employees.

At almost every step of the way, the leading brand has the advantage.

On an airplane flight, for example, the airline will often stock one brand of cola, one brand of ginger ale, one brand of beer, etc.

On your next flight, see if the three brands aren't Coke, Canada Dry and Budweiser. The three leading brands of cola, ginger ale and beer.

What makes a leader? Followers, of course. Leaders should not try to drive their competitors out of business. They need them to create a category. Polaroid made a serious mistake by suing Kodak and driving them out of the instant photography business. Both companies lost out.

Leadership is your best "differentiator." It's the collateral for your brand's success.

The Instability of Equality

It's true that in some categories the two leading brands run neck and neck.

What's equally true is that these categories are inherently unstable. Sooner or later, you can expect one brand to get the upper hand and open a lead which eventually will reach a stable 5 to 3 or 2 to 1 ratio.

Consumers are like chickens. They are much more

This thinking is what later led us to the "law of duality." In every category, there are two brands which will ultimately dominate the category. Chevrolet and Ford, Coke and Pepsi, Budweiser and Miller, Duracell and Energizer, Sotheby's and Christie's. God and the Devil.

comfortable with a pecking order that everybody knows about and accepts.

Hertz and Avis.

Harvard and Yale.

McDonald's and Burger King.

When two brands are close, one or the other is likely to get the upper hand and then dominate the market for years to come.

Between 1925 and 1930, for example, Ford and Chevrolet were locked in a head-to-head battle. Then Chevrolet took the lead in 1931. In the model years since, including dislocations caused by depression and wars, Chevrolet has lost the lead only four times.

The time for extra effort is clearly when the situation is in doubt. When neither side has a clear-cut superiority. Winning the battle for sales leadership in a single year will often clinch the victory for decades to come.

It takes 110 percent of rated power for a jet to get its wheels off the ground. Yet when it reaches 30,000 feet, the pilot can throttle back to 70 percent of power and still cruise at 600 miles per hour.

Strategies for Maintaining Leadership

Question: Where does the 800-pound gorilla sleep? Answer: Anywhere he wants to.

Leaders can do anything they want to. Short-term, leaders are almost invulnerable. Momentum alone carries them along. (Old wrestling expression: You can't get pinned when you're on top.)

For General Motors, Procter & Gamble and the leaders of this world, the worries are never about this year or next. Their worries are long-term. What's going to happen five years from now? Ten years from now? (Short-term, the only problem is the government. The motto of a leader ought to be: Keep pushing till you hear from the Feds.)

Leaders should use their short-term flexibility to assure themselves of a stable long-term future. As a matter of fact, the marketing leader is usually the one who moves the ladder into the mind with his or her brand nailed to the one and only rung. Once there, what should leaders do and not do?

Microsoft

Microsoft did just this and they did indeed hear from the Feds.

What Not to Do

As long as a company owns the position, there's no point in running ads that scream, "We're No. 1."

Much better is to enhance the product category in the prospect's mind. Notice IBM advertising usually ignores competition and sells the value of computers. All computers, not just the company's types.

Why isn't it a good idea to run advertising that says, "We're No. 1"?

The reason is pyschological. Either the prospect knows you are No. 1 and wonders why you are so insecure that you have to say so. Or the prospect doesn't know you are No. 1. If not, why not?

Maybe you have defined your leadership in your own terms and not the prospect's terms. Unfortunately, that just won't work.

Heineken

America's #1 imported beer.

We've had second thoughts about what leaders should not do. You always have new prospects coming into the marketplace who don't know what brand is the leader. Therefore leaders like Heineken should probably always run advertising to communicate their leadership. Unfortunately, Heineken dropped their line "America's No. 1 imported beer," and ultimately lost their leadership to Corona Extra. Leadership, however, should always be communicated with a certain amount of humility.

You can't build a leadership position on your own terms. "The best-selling under-$1,000 high-fidelity system east of the Mississippi."

You have to build a leadership position in the prospect's terms.

There are two basic strategies that should be used hand in hand. They seem contradictory but aren't.

The real thing.

Why Coke doesn't continue to use "The real thing" is beyond us. "Always Coke" was just wishful thinking. The current theme "Coca-Cola Enjoy" is childish.

Every product that gets into the mind first is perceived by the customer as the real thing. IBM in mainframe computers, Heinz in ketchup, Goodyear in tires and, of course, Coca-Cola in cola. When you are perceived as the real thing, you have also repositioned every other brand as an imitation. "The real thing" is perhaps the most powerful, most emotional advertising slogan ever invented, yet the Coca-Cola Company uses it sparingly, if at all. A pity.

Rubbing It In

"The real thing." This classic Coca-Cola advertising campaign is a strategy that can work for any leader.

The essential ingredient in securing the leadership position is getting into the mind first. The essential ingredient in keeping that position is reinforcing the original concept. The standard by which all others are judged. In contrast, everything else is an imitation of "the real thing."

This is not the same as saying "We're No. 1." The largest brand could be the largest seller because it has a lower price, it is available in more outlets, etc.

But "the real thing," like a first love, will always occupy a special place in the prospect's mind.

"We invented the product." A powerful motivating force behind Xerox copiers. Polaroid cameras. Zippo lighters.

Covering All Bets

Sometimes it's hard to do. Unfortunately, leaders often

read their own advertising so avidly they end up thinking they can do no wrong. So when a competitor introduces a new product or a new feature, the tendency is to pooh-pooh the development.

Leaders should do the opposite. They should cover all bets. This means a leader should swallow his or her pride and adopt every new product development as soon as it shows signs of promise. Too often, however, the leader doesn't wake up until it's too late.

General Motors spent $50 million to cover the Wankel engine when it was offered to the automotive industry. Money down the drain? Not necessarily. GM probably looks on the $50 million spent to buy a Wankel license as cheap insurance to protect a $66 billion business. (That's right, General Motors' sales in 1979 were $66,311,200,000.)

Suppose the Wankel had become the automotive engine of the future. And Ford or Chrysler had been the first to buy the rights. Where would General Motors be now?

Right where Kodak and 3M are in office copiers. When these two leaders in coated-paper copiers had a chance to cover by buying rights to Carlson's xerography process, they declined.

"Nobody would pay five cents for a plain-paper copy when they could get a coated-paper copy for a cent and a half." Logical enough. But the essence of covering is protection against the unexpected.

And the unexpected did happen. Haloid took a chance on the Carlson patents, and today the company (successively Haloid Xerox and then Xerox) is a

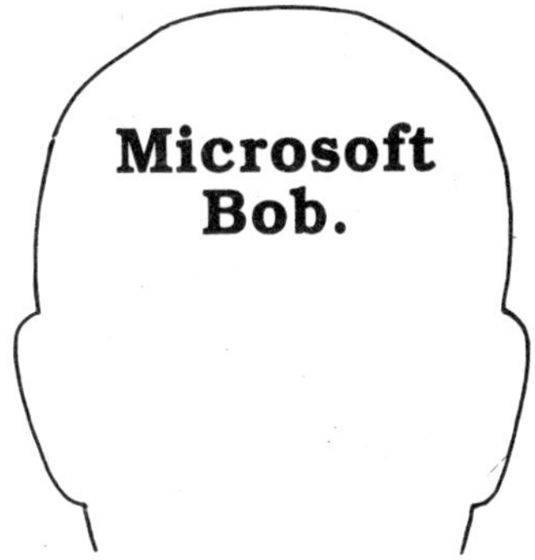

Leaders should take chances like Microsoft did with its Bob software, a product for the unsophisticated computer user. It failed, but what if a competitor had tried something similar and succeeded? Our experience is that most leaders suffer from hardening of the entrepreneurial arteries. They're too concerned with what the media might say if a new product failed. Yet the media is most sympathetic when you admit you made a mistake. Look at the great stories Coca-Cola received when they admitted that New Coke was a miscue.

$5 billion giant. Bigger than 3M and only a step behind Kodak. *Fortune* calls the Xerox 914 plain-paper copier "probably the single most profitable product ever manufactured in the United States."

And what did Xerox do for an encore?

Almost nothing. The spectacular success of the 914 was followed by one failure after another. Most notably in computers.

Today, of course, Xerox is much bigger than Kodak, which made the mistake of getting into pharmaceuticals and a host of other products. We later developed this line of thinking into the notion of the power of focusing.

Over a 20-year period Xerox lost several billion in computers. Another expensive lesson in the dangers of losing focus.

Power from the Product

"Only when our office copying success has been repeated, not once, but several times," said the Xerox chairman early on in the company's diversification game, "can we fairly reach the conclusion that this organization has the kind of power that can be relied upon again and again."

This is the classic mistake made by the leader. The illusion that the power of the product is derived from the power of the organization.

It's just the reverse. The power of the organization is derived from the power of the product. The position that the product owns in the prospect's mind.

Coca-Cola has power. The Coca-Cola Company is merely a reflection of that power.

Outside the cola field, the Coca-Cola Company has to earn its power the hard way. Either by getting into the mind first, by establishing a strong alternative position or by repositioning the leader.

So Coca-Cola's Mr. Pibb runs a poor second to Dr. Pepper, and all the power of the Coca-Cola Company can't do much about it.

So, too, with Xerox. The power is in the position that Xerox owns in the mind. Xerox means copier. Xerox owns the copier position because it got into the mind first and then exploited that copier position by a massive marketing program.

But in computers, office duplicators, word processors and other products, Xerox starts at ground zero. Xerox has obviously tried to duplicate its copier success in other fields. But it has apparently forgotten one essential element of the 914 program. It was the first to fly the plain-paper copier ocean.

We worked for Xerox for almost two years to try to get them to focus on the output side of the office (copiers, computer printers, etc.) rather than on the input side (computers). Specifically, we tried to get them to be the first company to introduce a desk-top laser printer. Unfortunately, they let Hewlett-Packard do just that.

Reacting Rapidly

When a competitor introduces a radically new concept, the reaction of red-blooded American management is predictable.

"Let's wait and see."

Yet time is of the essence if a covering move is to be effective. You want to block the competitor by moving aggressively to cover the new product before it becomes established in the prospect's mind.

When Datril tried a price attack on Tylenol, Johnson & Johnson immediately covered the move. They cut Tylenol's price. Even before Bristol-Myers started its Datril price advertising.

Result: Johnson & Johnson repelled the Datril attacks and inflicted heavy losses on the Bristol-Myers entry, which ended up with nothing to show for its efforts except a terrific headache.

Covering in a marketing race is not too different from covering in a sailboat race. Never let the oppo-

Another classic block was Gillette over BIC in disposable razors with their Good News twin-bladed disposable.

nent get out from under your sails and into the open water. You can't predict the future. You never know which way the wind will blow.

As long as the leader covers a competitive move, he or she will always be out in front. No matter which way the wind blows.

Covering with Multibrands

Tylenol is an exception. Most leaders should cover competitive moves by introducing another brand.

This is the classic "multibrand" strategy of Procter & Gamble. It may be a misnomer to call it a multibrand strategy. Rather it's a single-position strategy.

Each brand is uniquely positioned to occupy a certain location in the mind of the prospect. When times change, when new products come and go, no effort is made to change the position. Rather a new product is introduced to reflect changing technologies and changing tastes.

In other words, Procter & Gamble recognizes the enormous difficulty of moving an established position. When you have one already established, why change it? It may be cheaper and more effective in the long run to introduce a new product. Even if you eventually have to kill off an old, established name.

Ivory was a soap. It still is. When heavy-duty laundry detergents became available, the pressure was probably on to introduce Ivory Detergent. But this would have meant changing the position of Ivory in the prospect's mind.

Gillette
Trac II
Atra
Good News!
Sensor
Mach 3

Multiple brands are worth more in overall market share than single brands. (Gillette has a 60 share with its brands.)

LEXUS

One of the most brilliant examples of a multibrand strategy is Toyota's introduction of the Lexus. They didn't call the product a Super Toyota or a Toyota Ultra. No, they gave their expensive Toyotas a different brand name.

A much better solution was Tide. Now the new detergent concept had a new name to match. And Tide became an enormous success.

And when Procter & Gamble introduced a dishwasher detergent, they didn't call it Dishwasher Tide. They called it Cascade.

Each leading Procter & Gamble brand has its own separate identity: Joy, Crest, Head & Shoulders, Sure, Bounty, Pampers, Comet, Charmin and Duncan Hines. Not a Plus, Ultra or Super in the lot.

So a multibrand strategy is really a single-position strategy. One without change.

Ivory has been going strong for 99 years.

It was too good to last. For many years, Procter & Gamble was our hero. They launched a separate brand in each developing category. No longer. They have fallen into the conventional line-extension thinking. For example, they wound up with more than 50 SKUs of Crest toothpaste. No wonder Crest recently lost its leadership to Colgate.

Covering with a Broader Name

What dethrones a leader, of course, is change.

The New York Central Railroad was not only the leading railroad in the twenties, it was also the bluest of blue-chip stocks. Several mergers later, the Penn Central (as it is called today) is an anemic relic with scarcely a trace of its former glory.

American Airlines, on the other hand, is flying high.

The covering move for the New York Central, of course, would have been to open an airline division at an early stage in the game.

"What? You want us to start an airline to take business away from our railroad? Over my dead body we will."

The pure covering move is often difficult to sell

internally. Management often sees the new product or service as a competitor rather than as an opportunity.

Sometimes a name change will help bridge the gap from one era to the next. By broadening the name, you can allow the company to make the mental transition.

Sales Management, a 50-year-old publication, recently changed its name to *Sales Management and Marketing* to encompass the fast-growing function of marketing. At some point in the future the publication could drop the other shoe and change again. To *Marketing Management.*

From Haloid to Haloid Xerox to Xerox is the general pattern.

You know, of course, how the Kodak Company got its name. From Eastman to Eastman Kodak to Kodak, right?

The shoe has been dropped as "Eastman" was spun off with their chemical business.

Well, they haven't dropped the other shoe yet. So the official name is still the Eastman Kodak Company.

The Direct Mail Association changed its name a number of years ago to Direct Mail-Marketing Association. A recognition of the fact that mail was only one of the ways for a company to do direct marketing.

Is there any doubt that there's a Direct Marketing Association coming sometime in the future?

We should have added one important point. While the New York Central should have gotten intc the airline business, they definitely should not have used the New York Central name. In this situation, and many others, companies should think multibrands.

While a New York Central Transportation Company might not have been a success either, there is plenty of evidence to indicate that people take names very literally. (Eastern Airlines, for example.)

Government agencies are usually very good at the game of broadening the name. The Department of Housing and Urban Development, for example. (It used to be the Housing and Home Finance Agency.) By broadening the name, a government agency can enlarge its scope of operations, increase its staff and naturally justify a larger budget.

Oddly enough, one agency that missed a bet was the Federal Trade Commission. A broader name would be Consumer Protection Agency. A name that would also take advantage of a current hot topic.

Leaders can also benefit by broadening the range of applications for their products.

Arm & Hammer has done a good job in promoting the use of baking soda in the refrigerator.

And the new Florida Citrus Commission promotes orange juice, the largest-selling fruit drink, for lunch, snacks, with meals, etc. "It isn't just for breakfast anymore," say the commercials.

Business Week, the leading business magazine, has successfully promoted itself as a good publication for consumer advertising. Today roughly 40 percent of its advertising volume is in consumer products.

Consumer Protection Agency

This is a great idea, one so obvious that any 10-year-old would see its advantages. Why does a government that doesn't know how to run its own business effectively want to tell us what the ideal class size should be for a grade school?

The Benefits of Leadership

Unlike the famous Cadillac ad, "The penalty of leadership," there are enormous benefits of leadership.

The leader, the company with the highest market share, is also likely to enjoy the highest profit margin of any company serving that market. Look at the results of the four U.S. automotive companies in a typical year (1978).

General Motors had 49 percent of the market and net income of 6.1 percent on sales.

Oh, how the automotive world has changed. GM is down to 29 percent, Ford is 25 percent, Chrysler is now DaimlerChrysler with 17 percent and American Motors is gone.

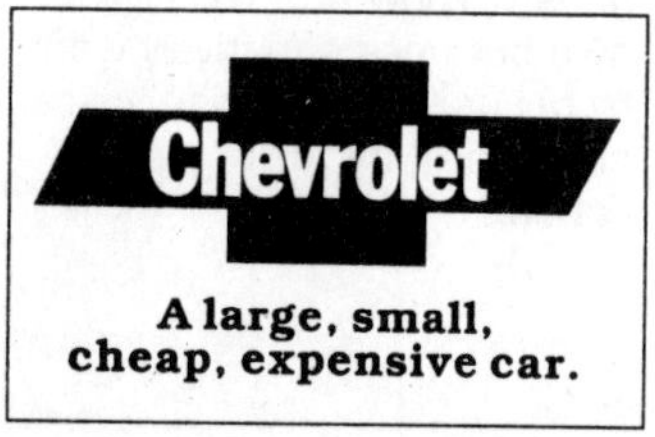

What's true in theory doesn't always work in practice. General Motors should be the dominant company in the automobile business with a market share in the neighborhood of 50 percent. Yet their market share has steadily declined to 29 percent. What went wrong? It's the positioning of the individual brands. What's a Chevrolet? A Chevrolet is a large, small, cheap, expensive car. When you try to be everything, you wind up being nothing. General Motors is making the same positioning mistake with the rest of its brands.

Ford had 34 percent of the market and net income of 4.4 percent.

Chrysler had 15 percent of the market and net income of 1.0 percent.

American Motors had 2 percent of the market and net income of 0.4 percent.

General Motors had 50 percent more net income than American Motors had sales.

The rich get richer and the poor get poorer.

Futhermore, the momentum created by this overwhelming leadership is bound to carry a company along for many years to come.

Note, too, it's not size that makes a company strong. It's mental position which contributes to market share that makes a company strong like General Motors. Or weak like Chrysler.

In sales, for example, Chrysler is twice the size of Procter & Gamble. But P & G is a leader in most of the categories it competes in. And Chrysler is a poor third.

As a result, Procter & Gamble is a very profitable company while Chrysler struggles to stay on the road.

The ultimate objective of a positioning program should be to achieve leadership in a given category. Once that leadership has been obtained, the company can count on enjoying the fruits of leadership for many years to come.

Getting to the top is tough. Staying there is much easier.

7 Positioning of a Follower

What works for a leader doesn't necessarily work for a follower. Leaders can often cover a competitive move and retain their leadership. (As Tylenol responded to the Datril price-cutting move.)

But followers are not in the same position to benefit from a covering strategy. When a follower copies a leader, it's not covering at all. It's better described as a me-too response. (Usually phrased more diplomatically as "keeping in tune with the times.")

Sometimes a me-too response can work for a follower. But only if the leader does not move rapidly enough to establish the position.

The Dangers of a Me-Too Response

Most me-too products fail to achieve reasonable sales goals because the accent is on "better" rather than "speed." That is, the No. 2 company thinks the road to success is to introduce a me-too product, only better.

It's not enough to be better than the competitor. You must launch your attack while the situation is fluid. Before the leader has time to establish leadership. With a more massive advertising and promotion launch. And a better name. (More on this point later.)

DEC spent a long time trying to "beat the IBM PC specs." They missed the desktop and got bought up by Compaq.

Yet the opposite normally occurs. The me-too company wastes valuable time on improving the product. Then the launch is made with a smaller advertising budget than the leader's. And then the new product is given the house name, because that's the easy way to ensure a quick share of market. All deadly traps in our overcommunicated society.

How do you find an open spot in the prospect's mind?

William Benton, founder, along with Chester Bowles, of the Benton & Bowles advertising agency, put it this way: "I would look for the soft spot in the business structure of the great corporations."

"Look for the hole" in the prospect's mind is one of the best strategies in the field of marketing. Creneaus don't have to be exciting or dramatic or even have much of a customer benefit to be effective. Rolex was the first expensive watch. Orville Redenbacher was the first expensive popcorn. Michelob was the first expensive domestic beer. Where is the customer benefit in being more expensive? Nevertheless, these brands were the first to fill these "holes" in the prospect's mind and all became very successful.

Cherchez le Creneau

The French have a marketing expression that sums up this strategy rather neatly.

Cherchez le creneau. "Look for the hole."

Cherchez le creneau and then fill it.

That advice goes against the "bigger and better" philosophy ingrained into the American spirit.

Another typically American attitude makes positioning thinking difficult. Ever since childhood, we have been taught to think in a certain way.

"The power of positive thinking," said Norman Vincent Peale. An attitude which may sell a lot of books but which can destroy a person's ability to find a creneau.

To find a creneau, you must have the ability to think in reverse, to go against the grain. If everyone else is going east, see if you can find your creneau by going west. A strategy that worked for Christopher Columbus can also work for you.

Let's explore some strategies for finding creneaus.

The Size Creneau

For years, Detroit automakers were on a longer, lower kick. Each model year, cars became more streamlined, better-looking.

Enter the Volkswagen Beetle. Short, fat and ugly.

The conventional way to promote the Beetle would have been to minimize the weaknesses and maximize the strengths.

"Let's get a fashion photographer who can make the car look better than it is. Then we'll play up the reliability angle," is your ordinary strategy.

But the creneau was size. The most effective ad Volkswagen ever ran was the one which stated the position clearly and unequivocally.

"Think small."

With two simple words, this headline did two things at once. It stated the Volkswagen position, and it challenged the prospect's assumption that bigger is necessarily better.

The effectiveness of this approach, of course, depends on the existence of an open creneau in the prospect's mind. Not that there weren't other small

Think small? Where's the benefit? Any decent research would have shown that most people wanted bigger cars than their neighbors. Yet it's more important in advertising to let prospects know what creneau you want to fill than it is to communicate some product benefit. Volkswagen's first job was to nail down the "small" hole in the mind.

cars on the market at the time the Beetle was introduced. There were, but no one else had preempted the small-car position.

Volkswagen is the classic example of establishing a creneau based on small size. Sony did the same thing in television. ("Tummy television.")

Integrated circuits and other electronic devices make the "small-size" creneau technically feasible in many product categories. Only time will tell which companies will be able to capitalize on electronics to build valuable positions based on miniaturization.

The opposite also presents opportunities too. Advent is building a position in large-size projection television, although the confusion of Advent television with Advent hi-fi speakers may tend to limit its success.

Advent invented projection television. Granted, projection TV with screen sizes of 40 to 60 inches never became more than a niche portion of a much larger TV market. But projection TV wasn't good enough for Bernie Mitchell, Advent's high-powered chief executive recruited from a successful run at Pioneer, the high-fidelity company. " Let's take Advent and branch out into the home entertainment center business," decided Mr. Mitchell. Of course, Advent wound up in bankruptcy court and the home entertainment center did, too, in a way. Another example of line extension run amok.

The High-Price Creneau

The classic example is Michelob. The people at Anheuser-Busch found an untapped market for a premium-priced domestic beer. And they moved into the mind with the Michelob name.

What's ironic about the Michelob story is that in theory, at least, there were many premium brands on the market. Schlitz, Budweiser and Pabst, to name three. (In fact, all three brands still carry the word "premium" on the label.) But time had eroded their premium position.

In the days of strong local brands (Schaefer in New York, Blatz in Milwaukee, Meister Brau in Chicago), the national or "shipping" brands were forced to

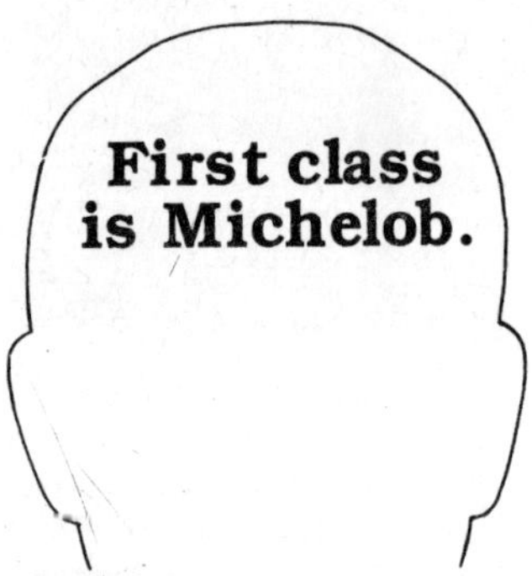

Michelob was launched with one of the great positioning lines of all time. Yet they rapidly abandoned it for such nonsensical concepts as "Weekends were made for Michelob."

charge a premium price. With decentralized breweries, this is no longer true. So time created a creneau which Michelob filled.

High-price creneaus seem to be opening up in many product categories. As our throwaway society sees the urgent need for conservation, there's a new appreciation of a quality product designed to last.

Which is one reason behind the success of $30,000 automobiles like the Mercedes Benz 450SL and BMW 633CSi.

Those $30,000 cars are now $75,000 cars and are as popular as ever.

And S. T. Dupont (nice name) lighters at, as the ads say, "$1,500 and down."

Price is an advantage, especially if you're the first in the category to establish the high-price creneau.

You don't have to be first to succeed, as long as you can create the perception that you were first. Chivas Regal continues to maintain its leadership in the high-priced Scotch category.

Chivas Regal scotch is a good example. There are other high-priced scotches such as Haig & Haig Pinch Bottle. But after World War II, they let their high-price positions decay. So when Chivas Regal moved in with a clear, obvious "we're the high-priced brand," it was hugely successful.

Now, of course, Chivas Regal is under attack from Johnny Walker Black Label and Cutty 12. But the first brand into the mind, Chivas Regal, is in a strong position. Especially when the attacking brands have weak names that are easily confused with the house names, Johnny Walker and Cutty Sark.

Some brands base almost their entire product message on the high-price concept.

"There is only one Joy, the costliest perfume in the world."

"Why you should invest in a Piaget, the world's most expensive watch."

Mobil 1 has not done particularly well. The concept (first synthetic engine lubricant) is brilliant, but the name is a dud. A new concept needs a new name, not a synthetic line-extension name. Oddly enough, synthetic motor oils have done well in Europe, but not in the United States. One reason: No company here has introduced a major brand of synthetic motor oil with a new, synthetic-only brand name. This is still a category waiting for a leader to take charge.

Your high price must have a real difference to justify the price. If nothing else, it rationalizes the spending of more money.

High price is effective not only for luxury items like cars, scotch, perfume and watches, but also mundane products like popcorn. Orville Redenbacher's Gourmet Popping Corn at 89 cents a jar is taking a significant share of market away from such brands as Jolly Time at half the price.

Mobil 1 synthetic engine lubricant at $3.95 a quart is another example. Even traditional low-priced products like flour, sugar and salt represent positioning opportunities.

Too often, however, greed gets confused with positioning thinking. Charging high prices is not the way to get rich. Being the first to (1) establish the high-price position (2) with a valid product story (3) in a category where consumers are receptive to a high-priced brand is the secret of success. Otherwise, your high price just drives prospective customers away.

Furthermore, the place to establish the high price is in the ads, not in the store. The price (high or low) is as much a feature of the product as anything else.

If you do your positioning job right, there should be no price surprises in the store. Your ads don't have to quote exact prices, although sometimes that's a good thing to do. What they should do, however, is to clearly position your brand in a particular price category.

The Low-Price Creneau

Instead of high price, the opposite direction can also be a profitable tack to take.

Currently, the largest-volume brand of facsimile equipment is Qwip, made by an Exxon subsidiary. Qwip fax units at $29 a month and up compete with Xerox telecopiers at $45 a month and up. Currently, Qwip is placing as many fax units on rental as the rest of the industry combined.

In evaluating price as a possible creneau, keep in mind that the low-price creneau is often a good choice for new products like facsimile equipment and videotape players. Products customers believe they are taking a chance on. (If the thing doesn't work right, I'm not out that much money.)

The high-price creneau is often a good choice for old, established products like automobiles, watches and television sets. Especially those products for which customers are not happy with existing repair services.

The recent introduction of generic ("no name") food brands is an attempt to exploit the low-price creneau in the supermarket. (Although retailer emphasis on sales and low prices over the years have pretty much wiped out the opportunities in that direction.)

When you combine all three price strategies (high, standard and low), you normally have a strong marketing approach. As Anheuser-Busch has done with Michelob, Budweiser and Busch (their low-priced beer).

The weakest brand, of course, is Busch because of the poor name and lack of a strong positioning concept. Why would the owner of the place put his name

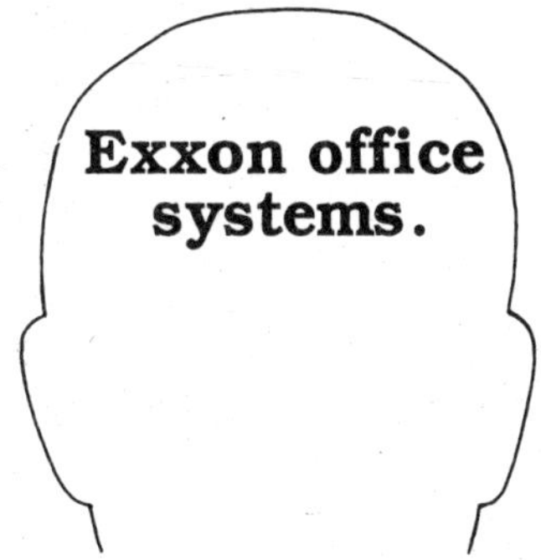

What happened to Qwip? The company decided to market a full line of office equipment products under the Exxon name. This turned out to be a major faux pas. The office systems division was folded after running up a river of red ink. What does a gasoline company know about office products anyway?

only on his lowest-priced product? This name problem plagues the Ford Motor Company too, with its Lincolns, Mercurys and Fords.

Other Effective Creneaus

Calvin Klein jeans were another example of a successful positioning program using sex.

Study old cigarette advertisements. It's hard to find an old cigarette ad that doesn't include women. This is astounding, since the cigarette market was primarily male. As a result, all cigarette brands became unisex brands in an attempt to broaden the market. Phillip Morris did the opposite. They threw out the women and focused on men. Then they decided to focus on the cowboy, a man's man. As a result of this positioning strategy, Marlboro became the largest selling cigarette in the world.

Sex is one. Marlboro was the first national brand to establish a masculine position in cigarettes, one reason why Phillip Morris's Marlboro brand has climbed steadily in sales. From fifth place in sales to first place in a 10-year period.

Timing is critical. In 1973 Lorillard tried to introduce its own masculine brand called Luke. The name was terrific, the packaging was great, the advertising was brilliant. "From Kankakee to Kokomo along comes Luke movin' free and slow."

The only thing wrong was the timing. About 20 years too late. Luke really was movin' slow, so Lorillard killed him.

In positioning a product, there's no substitute for getting there first.

What masculinity did for Marlboro, femininity did for Virginia Slims, a brand that carved out a substantial share with the opposite approach. But Eve, a me-too brand that also tried the feminine approach, was a failure.

When you use sex to segment a product category and establish a position, the obvious approach isn't always the best.

Take perfume, for example. You'd think that the more delicate and feminine the brand, the more successful it would be. So what's the largest-selling brand of perfume in the world?

No, it's not Arpege or Chanel No. 5. It's Revlon's Charlie. The first brand to try a masculine name complete with pantsuit ads.

The knockoff brand, "Just Call Me Maxi," was not only poorly done but reportedly cost the president of Max Factor his job.

The Charlie success story illustrates the paradox of established product categories like perfume. The bulk of the business is in one direction (feminine brand names), but the opportunity lies in the opposite (a masculine-directed brand name).

Age is another positioning strategy to use. Geritol tonic is a good example of a successful product aimed at older folks.

Aim toothpaste is a good example of a product aimed at children. Aim has carved out 10 percent of the toothpaste market. A tremendous accomplishment in a market dominated by two powerful brands, Crest and Colgate.

Time of day is also a potential positioning possibility. Nyquil, the first night-time cold remedy, is one example.

Distribution is another possibility. L'eggs was the first hosiery brand to be distributed in supermarkets and mass merchandise outlets. L'eggs now is the leading brand, with sales in the hundreds of millions.

Another possibility is the heavy-user position. "The one beer to have when you're having more than one" positioned Schaefer as the brand for the heavy

Nothing lasts forever, especially in categories that are "fashion" oriented. Perfume, clothing, liquor, etc. Charlie was replaced by a host of newer perfume brands. In clothing, for example, Calvin Klein was superseded by Ralph Lauren, who is in the process of losing out to Tommy Hilfiger. With a multiple-brand strategy, a company can keep on top of its market by launching new brands at the appropriate time. Younger people are leaving Levi's and buying hipper brands like FUBU and Diesel. "They don't want to wear what their parents wear." Levi Strauss should launch a second brand of blue jeans designed for the children of its current customers.

"Hey, Mom, kids will brush longer because they love the taste." Aim moved away from this kid strategy and their 10 percent share went to a 0.8 percent share. As we said earlier, use it or lose it.

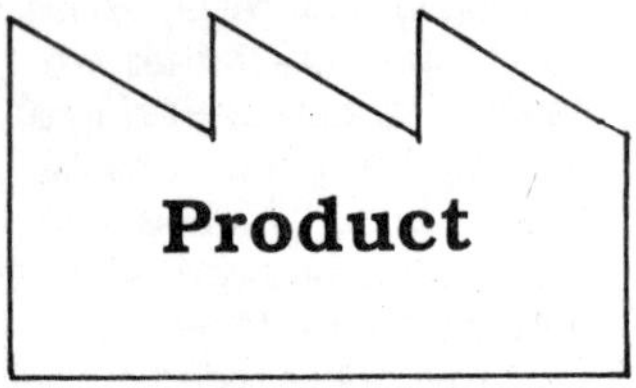

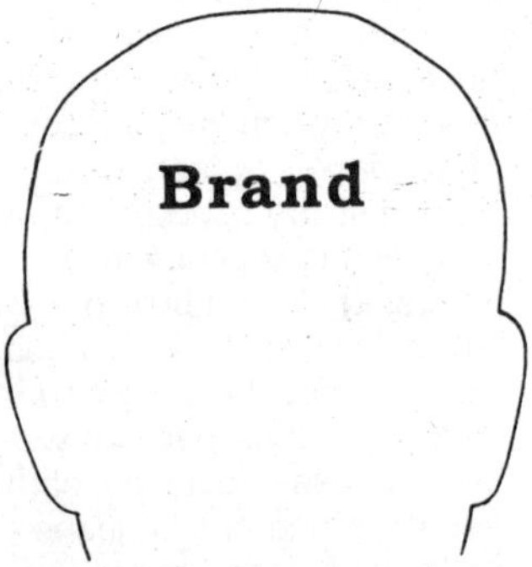

Even today, companies are focused on building products rather than brands. A product is something made in a factory. A brand is something made in the mind. To be successful today, you have to build brands, not products. And you build brands by using positioning strategies, starting with a good name. Any automobile brand named "Edsel" is bound to run off the road.

beer drinker. When the Schaefer campaign started almost two decades ago, there were five breweries in the city of New York. Today there is just one left. Schaefer.

The Factory Creneau

One common mistake in looking for creneaus is filling a hole in the factory rather than one in the mind.

Ford's Edsel is the classic example. In the laughter that followed the demise of poor Edsel, most people missed the point.

In essence, the Ford people got switched around. The Edsel was a beautiful case of internal positioning to fill a hole between Ford and Mercury on the one hand and Lincoln on the other hand.

Good strategy inside the factory. Bad strategy outside where there was simply no position for this car in a category already cluttered with heavily chromed, medium-priced cars.

If the Edsel had been tagged a "high-performance" car and presented in a sleek two-door, bucket-seat form and given a name to match, no one would have laughed. It could have occupied a position that no one else owned, and the ending of the story might have been different.

Another "fill-the-factory" mistake was the *National Observer,* the first national weekly newspaper.

Dow Jones, the *Observer*'s proud parent, also publishes *The Wall Street Journal,* but only five days a week. Voilà, you can hear somebody say. Let's fill the factory with a weekly newspaper. That way, we get free use of those expensive *Journal* presses.

But where was the hole in the prospect's mind? He or she could already subscribe to *Time, Newsweek, U.S. News & World Report* and other news magazines.

Aah, you say. But the *National Observer* is a weekly newspaper, not a magazine. And another semantic victory is won at the expense of losing the marketing war.

The Technology Trap

Even a great technical achievement of a research laboratory will fail if there is no creneau in the mind.

In 1971 Brown-Forman Distillers launched Frost 8/80, the first "dry, white whisky."

Frost 8/80 should have been a big success. There was a big hole there. There was no other dry, white whisky. As Brown-Forman president William F. Lucas said, "It was greeted with great applause by our people and a gnashing of teeth by our competitors."

Yet less than two years later, Frost 8/80 was dead. A multimillion-dollar failure. Volume had totaled just 100,000 cases, one-third of the company's projections.

What went wrong? Look at the positioning claim from the prospect's point of view.

The first white whisky? Not true. There are at least four others. Their names are gin, vodka, rum and tequila.

As a matter of fact, Frost 8/80 ads encouraged the prospect to look at the new whisky as a substitute for other distilled spirits. According to the ads, Frost 8/80 could be used like vodka or gin in martinis, like scotch or bourbon in manhattans and whisky sours.

Positioning is not a game for the simple-minded. Yes, white whisky is a first in the bottle, but it's not a first in the mind where it really counts. Whisky is brown in the mind. How can you have a white whisky? Frost 8/80 was no more successful than Miller Clear, the first white beer, or Crystal Pepsi, the first white cola. Beer is light brown and cola is reddish brown. When you tamper with these colors in the mind, you are trying to change deeply held perceptions. Don't bother. They never learn. Currently, Heinz is trying to introduce a green ketchup. Ketchup in the mind is red.

Don't play semantic games with the prospect. Advertising is not a debate. It's a seduction.

The prospect won't sit still for the finer points of verbal logic. As the politician said, "If it looks like a duck and walks like duck, I say it's a duck."

The biggest single mistake that companies make is trying to appeal to everybody. The everybody trap. Rather than asking yourself, "Who are we trying to appeal to?" try asking yourself the opposite question, "Who should not use our brand?" Most companies find that their strategies really do not rule out anybody. If you don't sacrifice, you can't win in today's highly competitive marketing arena.

The Everybody Trap

Some marketing people reject the "cherchez le creneau" concept. They don't want to be tied down to a specific position because they believe it limits their sales. Or their opportunities.

They want to be all things to all people.

Years ago, when there were a lot fewer brands and a lot less advertising, it made sense to try to appeal to everybody.

In politics it used to be suicide for a politician to take a strong position on anything. Don't step on anybody's toes.

But today in the product arena and in the political arena, you have to have a position. There are too many competitors out there. You can't win by not making enemies, by being everything to everybody.

To win in today's competitive environment, you have to go out and make friends, carve out a specific niche in the market. Even if you lose a few doing so.

Today the everybody trap may keep you afloat if you're already in office or already own a substantial share of market. But it's deadly if you want to build a position from nowhere.

8 Repositioning the Competition

There comes a time when you can't find a creneau. With hundreds of variations in each product category on the market, the chances of finding an open hole today are very slim.

For example, take your average supermarket today. It has 10,000 different products or brands on display. That means a young person has to sort out and catalog 10,000 different names in his or her head.

When you consider that the average college graduate has a speaking vocabulary of only 8,000 words, you can see the problem.

The kid spends four years in a university and ends up 2,000 words down.

Creating Your Own Creneau

With a plethora of products in every category, how does a company use advertising to blast its way into the mind? The basic underlying marketing strategy has got to be "reposition the competition."

Another example of the power of being first: What's the name of the second sea captain to lead an expedition to the New World? In 1497, five years after Columbus's first voyage, John Cabot led an English expedition which eventually reached the Gulf of St. Lawrence. When Cabot returned to London, King Henry promptly presented him with a miserable 10 pounds. No fame, no fortune, no favorable mentions in the history books for an explorer who's No. 2.

Because there are so few creneaus to fill, a company must create one by repositioning the competitors that occupy the positions in the mind.

In other words, to move a new idea or product into the mind, you must first move an old one out.

"The world is round," said Christopher Columbus. "No, it's not," said the public, "it's flat."

To convince the public otherwise, fifteenth-century scientists first had to prove that the world wasn't flat.

One of their more convincing arguments was the fact that sailors at sea were first able to observe the tops of the masts of an approaching ship, then the sails, then the hull. If the world were flat, they would see the whole ship at once.

All the mathematical arguments in the world weren't as effective as a simple observation the public could verify themselves.

Once an old idea is overturned, selling the new idea is often ludicrously simple. As a matter of fact, people will often actively search for a new idea to fill the void.

Never be afraid of conflict either. The crux of a repositioning program is undercutting an existing concept, product or person.

Conflict, even personal conflict, can build a reputation overnight.

Where would Sam Ervin have been without Richard Nixon?

For that matter, where would Richard Nixon have been without Alger Hiss?

And Ralph Nader got famous not by saying anything about Ralph Nader but by going out and attacking the world's largest corporation single-handedly.

People like to watch the bubble burst.

Repositioning Aspirin

Tylenol went out and burst the aspirin bubble.

"For the millions who should not take aspirin," said Tylenol's ads. "If your stomach is easily upset . . . or you have an ulcer . . . or you suffer from asthma, allergies or iron-deficiency anemia, it would make good sense to check with your doctor before you take aspirin.

"Aspirin can irritate the stomach lining," continued the Tylenol ad, "trigger asthmatic or allergic reactions, cause small amounts of hidden gastrointestinal bleeding.

"Fortunately, there is Tylenol . . ."

Sixty words of copy before any mention of the advertiser's product.

Sales of Tylenol acetaminophen took off. Today Tylenol is the No. 1 brand of analgesic. Ahead of Anacin. Ahead of Bayer. Ahead of Bufferin. Ahead of Excedrin. A simple but effective repositioning strategy did the job.

Against an institution like aspirin. Amazing.

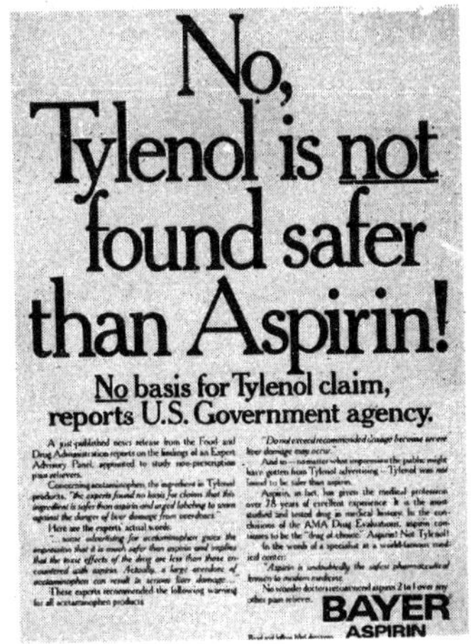

Bayer tried to fight back with an advertising campaign that took issue with the Tylenol claims. Not a good idea. It legitimized the Tylenol message. The prospect thought: "If Bayer aspirin is so worried about Tylenol that they have to run a million-dollar advertising campaign to refute those claims, there must be something to the notion that aspirin causes stomach bleeding."

Today, the No. 2 brand is Advil. "Advanced medicine for pain" repositioned the entire category.

Repositioning Lenox

For a repositioning strategy to work, you must say something about your competitor's product that causes the prospect to change his or her mind, not about your product, but about the competitor's product.

"Royal Doulton. The china of Stoke-on-Trent, England versus Lenox. The china of Pomona, New Jersey."

Note how Royal Doulton is repositioning Lenox china, a product that many buyers thought was an imported one. (Lenox? Sounds English, doesn't it?)

Royal Doulton credits a 6 percent gain in market share to this one advertisement.

The late Howard Gossage used to say that the objective of your advertising should not be to communicate with your consumers and prospects at all, but to terrorize your competition's copywriters, and there's some truth in that.

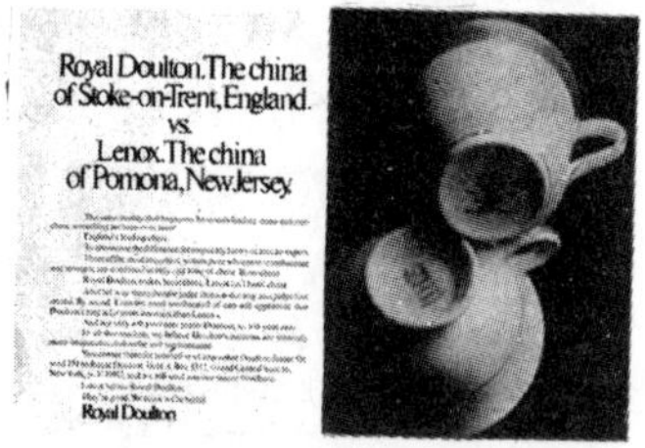

It's not enough to say that your product (Royal Doulton) is fine English china. The competitive brand (Lenox) was first in the mind. With a name like Lenox, prospects thought the product came from England. Royal Doulton repositioned Lenox where they really belonged, in Pomona, New Jersey.

Repositioning American Vodkas

"Most American vodkas seem Russian," said the ads. And the captions said: "Samovar: Made in Schenley, Pennsylvania. Smirnoff: Made in Hartford, Connecticut. Wolfschmidt: Made in Lawrenceburg, Indiana.

"Stolichnaya is different. It is Russian," continued the ad. And the bottle is labeled, "Made in Leningrad, Russia."

Stolichnaya sales began to soar as a result. Needless to say.

But why the need to disparage the competition? Couldn't Pepsico, the importers of the Stolichnaya brand, have simply advertised it as the "Russian vodka?"

They could have, of course. But that presumes a

degree of product interest on the part of the vodka buyer that just doesn't exist.

Stolichnaya grabbed the Russian vodka position and then during the Afghanistan crisis started to have cold feet. They backed off their Russian claim and started running advertising that didn't mention their Russian heritage. As a result, they left an opening for Absolut, which moved into the vodka market and captured the leadership position, which it still holds today.

How many times have you picked up a bottle of liquor and read the label to find out where it was made? Furthermore, the names themselves (Samovar, Smirnoff, Wolfschmidt, Popov, Nikolai) imply a Russian origin. It's this latter factor alone that was responsible for much of Stolichnaya's astounding success.

People like to see the high and mighty exposed. They like to see those bubbles burst. (Which is what happened to Evening in Paris perfume.)

Note, too, how the advertising for other vodka brands plays into Stolichnaya's hands.

> It was the Golden Age of Russia. Yet in this time when legends lived, the Czar stood like a giant among men. He could bend an iron bar on his bare knee. Crush a silver ruble with his fist. And had a thirst for life like no other man alive. And his drink was Genuine Vodka. Wolfschmidt Vodka.

Then the reader turns the page to find the Stolichnaya ad, where he sees that Wolfschmidt is made in Lawrenceburg, Indiana.

Along comes Afghanistan and suddenly Stolichnaya is in trouble. But only temporarily. Assuming we don't go to war with Russia, the storm will blow over and Stolichnaya will come back bigger than ever.

Repositioning Pringle's

What happened to Pringle's potato chips? Introduced

with a $15 million fanfare from Procter & Gamble, the "new-fangled" potato chips rapidly gobbled up 18 percent of the market.

Then the old-fangled brands like Borden's Wise struck back with a classic repositioning strategy.

They read the labels on television.

"In Wise, you find: Potatoes. Vegetable oil. Salt.

"In Pringle's, you find: Dehydrated potatoes. Mono- and di-glycerides. Ascorbic acid. Butylated hydroxy-anisole."

Sales of Pringle's came tumbling down. From a respectable 18 percent of the potato chip market to 10 percent. A far cry from P & G's goal of 25 percent.

Oddly enough, research isolated another problem. The most common complaint against Pringle's is that they "taste like cardboard."

It's exactly what you might expect from a consumer exposed to words like "di-glycerides" and "butylated hydroxy-anisole." Taste, esthetic or gustatory, is in the mind. Your eyes see what you expect to see. Your tongue reacts the way you expect it to react.

If you were forced to drink a beaker of di-hydrogen oxide, your response would probably be negative. If you asked for a glass of water, you might enjoy it.

That's right. There's no difference on the palate. The difference is in the brain.

Recently the Cincinnati giant changed its strategy. Pringle's would become an "all natural" product.

But the damage had already been done. In politics or packaged goods, the rule is once a loser, always a loser. It's just as hard to bring Pringle's back as it would be to bring Bella Abzug back.

We were wrong. It took a while, but Pringle's did come back with a strategy that emphasized their real difference, the packaging. Pringle's, however, was never able to achieve the market leadership goal that Procter & Gamble had in mind when they launched the brand.

Pringle's is still nowhere in a category dominated by Lay's and Ruffles.

In some small corner of the brain is a penalty box marked "loser." Once your product is sent there, the game is over.

Go back to square one and start all over again. With a new product and a new game.

Of all companies, Procter & Gamble should have known the power of repositioning. And have taken steps in advance to protect Pringle's.

Before the launch of Scope, we are quite sure that market research would have shown little acceptance of a mouthwash that didn't "taste bad." Yet Procter & Gamble went against conventional mouthwash thinking by launching a good-tasting brand. Good strategy for a product and good strategy for a positioning campaign. You never know what will work until you try it. As long as you have figured out a unique position, you have a chance to develop a successful brand.

Repositioning Listerine

One of P&G's most powerful programs is the one for Scope mouthwash. P&G used two words to reposition Listerine, the King of Halitosis Hill.

"Medicine breath."

These two words were enough to torpedo Listerine's highly successful "the taste you hate, twice a day" theme.

The Scope attack carved a few share points out of market leader Listerine and firmly established Scope in second place.

The Listerine/Scope battle caused the usual casualties. Micrin and Binaca folded. Lavoris saw its market share wither away. (Old African proverb: When elephants fight, it's the ants that get hurt.)

But let's face it. Scope has not become the market success it should be, based on theory.

Why? Look at the name again.

Scope? It sounds like a board game from Parker Brothers. Not like a good-tasting mouthwash that will make you a big hit with the opposite sex. If Scope had been given a name like Close-Up toothpaste, it could

We were wrong about the name. Scope is now neck and neck with Listerine. A better name, however, might have made Scope the dominant mouthwash brand.

have parlayed its brilliant repositioning strategy with sales success to match.

Repositioning vs. Comparative Ads

The success of the Tylenol, Scope, Royal Doulton and other repositioning programs has spawned a host of similar advertising. Too often, however, these copycat campaigns have missed the essence of repositioning strategy.

Look at this Royal Crown advertisement, which claims that one million taste tests show that Royal Crown beats Coca-Cola 57 percent to 43 percent. Also that Royal Crown beats Pepsi-Cola 53 percent to 47 percent. Why don't people believe advertisements like this? They say to themselves, "If Royal Crown tasted better than Coke and Pepsi, Royal Crown would be the leading brand. Since it isn't, it can't taste better."

"We're better than our competitors" isn't repositioning. It's comparative advertising and not very effective. There's a psychological flaw in the advertiser's reasoning which the prospect is quick to detect. "If you're so smart, how come you're not rich?"

Which is the typical viewer response to the "Pepsi Challenge." Pepsi-Cola commercials claimed that more than half the Coke drinkers prefer Pepsi.

Actually, Pepsi gained a few share points in Dallas, where the first Pepsi challenge commercials ran. But it was so far behind Coke that those few points were insignificant in closing the gap.

In New York, the country's biggest soft-drink market, Coca-Cola even gained a few points after the Pepsi challenge began running.

A look at other comparative ads suggests why most of them aren't effective. They fail to reposition the competition.

Rather, they use the competitor as a benchmark for their own brand. Then they tell the reader or viewer how much better they are. Which, of course, is exactly what the prospect expects the advertiser to say.

"Ban is more effective than Right Guard, Secret, Sure, Arrid Extra Dry, Mitchum, Soft & Dry, Body All, and Dial," said a recent Ban ad (which should have been banned itself).

This Ban advertisement is a comparative ad, but not a repositioning one. As a result, it is totally ineffective in establishing a position for Ban in comparison with all the other deodorants in the field. When prospects look at advertisements like this one, they add the words, "In the opinion of the manufacturer, Ban is more effective than . . ." It would not seem illogical to the average person to see a similar ad that said, "Right Guard is more effective than . . ."

Is Repositioning Legal?

If disparagement were illegal, every politician would be in jail. (And many husbands and wives would be in deep trouble too.)

Actually, the Federal Trade Commission deserves much of the credit for making repositioning ads possible. At least on television.

In 1964 the National Broadcasting Company dropped its ban on comparative advertising. But nothing much happened. Commercials are expensive to produce, and few advertisers wanted to produce two versions. One to run on NBC and one to run on the other two networks.

So in 1972 the FTC prodded the American Broadcasting Company and the Columbia Broadcasting System to allow comercials that named rival brands.

In 1974 the American Association of Advertising Agencies issued new comparative ad guidelines which represented a complete turnaround from previous policy. Traditionally, the 4A's had discouraged the use of comparative ads by its member agencies.

In 1975 the Independent Broadcasting Authority, which controls radio and television in Britain, gave the green light for "knocking" ads in the U.K.

When Michael Pertschuk, the current FTC chairman, was asked if he was opposed to ads that mention

When you run a repositioning campaign, you want to be "fair." That is, you should treat the competition in an ethical way. Ragu was (and still is) the leading spaghetti sauce. Their share, however, has declined substantially because Prego has successfully positioned itself as the "thick" spaghetti sauce. (Prego television commercials compared the two brands by name.) One reason this is effective is that "thin" spaghetti sauce isn't necessarily bad. Italian (or Old World Style) spaghetti sauce is a thin sauce. Take your choice. If you want thin sauce, reach for the Ragu. If you want thick sauce, go for the Prego.

competitors, he replied, "Absolutely not. We think they're great."

Is Repositioning Ethical?

In the past advertising was prepared in isolation. That is, you studied the product and its features, and then you prepared advertising which communicated to your customers and prospects the benefits of those features. It didn't make much difference whether the competition offered those features or not.

In the traditional approach, you ignored competition and made every claim seem like a preemptive claim. Mentioning a competitive product, for example, was considered not only bad taste but poor strategy as well.

In the positioning era, however, the rules are reversed. To establish a position, you must often not only name competitive names but also ignore most of the old advertising rules as well.

In category after category, the prospect already knows the benefits of using the product. To climb on his or her product ladder, you must relate your brand to the brands already there.

Yet repositioning programs, even though effective, have stirred up a host of complaints. Many advertising people deplore the use of such tactics.

An old-time advertising man put it this way. "Times have changed. No longer are advertisers content to huckster their own wares on their own merits. Their theme now is how much better their product is than any other. It is a deplorable situation, with TV as the worst offender, where competitive products are pictured and denigrated before the eyes of millions. There should be some kind of regulation to restrict that type of unethical marketing."

"Comparative advertising is not against the law," said the chairman of a top 10 agency, "nor should it be. But to practice it as we do today makes a mockery of pretensions to culture and refinement and decent corporate behavior."

Maybe so. Napoleon broke the rules of civilized warfare, and history hailed him a military genius.

Culture and refinement may be admirable qualities, but not in advertising war.

Is society sick when people are ready to believe the worst about a product or person, but balk about believing the best?

Are newspapers wrong to put the bad news on the front page and the good news in the back along with the society columns? (If they print any at all.)

The communication industry is like gossip. It feeds on the bad news, not the good.

It may not be your idea of the way things should be. It just happens to be the way things are.

To be successful in this overcommunicated society of ours, you have to play the game by the rules that society sets. Not your own.

Don't be discouraged. A little disparagement may be preferable in the long run to a lot of conventional "brag and boast."

Done honestly and fairly, it keeps the competition on their toes.

Before Burger King's brilliant "Have it your way"

Have it your way.

BURGER KING

repositioning campaign, the people at McDonald's were content to serve their hamburgers only one way. The McDonald's way. Now even Ronald can get a burger at his place "without pickles and without ketchup."

Now if only someone would open up a place that serves hamburgers "without kids."

Like all effective repositioning campaigns, the Burger King message was a "two-sided" affair. On the one hand, Burger King said that you could get your hamburger tailor-made at their place. On the other hand, the implication was that McDonald's was faster because the product was standardized. No one approach can appeal to everybody. As a matter of fact, Burger King dropped this program precisely because it slowed up the service. Burger King's next campaign was also a repositioning effort called "broiling, not frying" which went on to become the most effective program the company had ever run. "It was developed out of the thinking which resulted from reading your book," Jeff Campbell, president of Burger King, wrote to us in 1982. Subsequently, Campbell hired us to develop a follow-up strategy. Read the last line of this chapter again. We suggested that Burger King position themselves as the place for older kids, not the 2- to 6-year-olds that hang out at Mickey D's. "Grow up to the flame-broiled taste of Burger King" was the theme. At the client's suggestion, we took the Grow Up program to their advertising agency, which proceeded to dump all over the idea. It was one of the major disappointments of our life that this program was never used.

9 The Power of the Name

The name is the hook that hangs the brand on the product ladder in the prospect's mind. In the positioning era, the single most important marketing decision you can make is what to name the product.

Shakespeare was wrong. A rose by any other name would not smell as sweet. Not only do you see what you want to see, you also smell what you want to smell. Which is why the single most important decision in the marketing of perfume is the name you decide to put on the brand.

Would "Alfred" have sold as well as "Charlie?" Don't bet on it.

And Hog Island in the Caribbean was going nowhere until they changed its name to Paradise Island.

How to Choose a Name

Don't look to the past for guidance and pick the name of a French racing car driver (Chevrolet) or the daughter of your Paris representative (Mercedes).

Lite had the enormous advantage of being the first light beer in the mind, yet the generic name turned out to be a serious disadvantage. Renamed Miller Lite, the brand currently is a poor second to Bud Light and will probably lose out to Coors Light, too.

What worked in the past won't necessarily work now or in the future. In the past when there were fewer products, when the volume of communication was lower, the name wasn't nearly as important.

Today, however, a lazy, say-nothing name isn't good enough to cut into the mind. What you must look for is a name that begins the positioning process. A name that tells the prospect what the product's major benefit is.

Like Head & Shoulders shampoo, Intensive Care skin lotion, Slender diet drink and Close-Up toothpaste.

Or like DieHard for a longer-lasting battery. Shake 'n Bake for a new way to cook chicken. Edge for a shaving cream that lets you shave closer.

A name should not go "over the edge," though. That is, become so close to the product itself that it becomes generic, a general name for all products of its class rather than a trade name for a specific brand.

"Lite beer from Miller" is a typical product name that went over the line. So now we have Schlitz Light, Anheuser-Busch Natural Light and a host of other light beers. The public and the press quickly corrupted the name to "Miller Lite," and so Miller lost its right to exclusive use of "light" or its phonetic equivalent as a trademark for beer.

Availability of names is today's No. 1 trademark problem. There are 1.6 million registered trademarks in the United States. In Europe there are 3 million. It's often easier to buy one than to find one.

For years to come, trademark attorneys will be using Lite as an example of the danger of using descriptive words as trademarks. (Lawyers love coined names like Kodak and Xerox.)

Choosing a name is like driving a racing car. To win, you have to take chances. You have to select names that are almost, but not quite, generic. If once in a while you go off the track into generic territory, so be it. No world champion driver has made it to the top without spinning out a few times.

A strong, generic-like, descriptive name will block your me-too competitors from muscling their way into your territory. A good name is the best insurance for long-term success. *People* is a brilliant name for a gossip-column magazine. It's a runaway success. The me-too copy, *Us* magazine, is in trouble.

How Not to Choose a Name

On the other hand, *Time* is not as good a name for a newsweekly as the more generic *Newsweek*.

Time was the first into the newsweekly pool and is an obvious success. But *Newsweek* isn't far behind. (As a matter of fact, *Newsweek* sells more pages of advertising each year than does *Time*.)

Many people think *Time* is a great name for a magazine. And in a way, it is. Short, catchy, memorable. But it's also subtle and tricky. (*Time* could be a trade magazine for the watch industry.)

Fortune is another name cut out of the same cloth. (*Fortune* could be a magazine for stockbrokers, commodity traders or gamblers. It's not clear.) *Business Week* is a much better name. Also a much more successful magazine.

Names also get out of date, opening up creneaus for alert competitors.

Esquire was a great name for a magazine for the young-man-about-town. When young-men-about-

TIME

Newsweek

We'll have to eat crow on this one. Today we think the brand name *Time* is a better name than the generic name *Newsweek*. We also think that *Fortune* is a better name than *Business Week*. We were misled by the obvious success of the two magazines with generic names. In the magazine field, there are such "barriers of entry" that a generic name is not the liability that it would be in, let's say, the package goods field. In a supermarket or drugstore, a new category generally attracts a raft of generic products which cause a lot of confusion. A brand with a generic name seldom becomes a big seller.

PLAYBOY

MAXIM

Words get worn out. Today's playboys would never call themselves "playboys," creating an opportunity for a new magazine for young males. The big winner is *Maxim*, selected by *Advertising Age* as its magazine of the year. No brand will live forever. Products get out of date, services get out of date, even names get out of date. The smart company will not waste money defending the past, but rather will launch new brands to take advantage of the opportunities created by change. *Playboy* should have launched a publication with a name like *Maxim*. They should not have let someone else do it to them.

town used to sign their names John J. Smith, Esq. But *Esquire* lost its leadership to *Playboy*. Everybody knows what a playboy is and what he's interested in. Girls, right? But what's an esquire? And what's he interested in?

For many years, *Yachting* has been the leading publication in the marine field. But today how many esquires own yachts? And so we predict that *Yachting* will find itself overtaken by magazines like *Sail*.

When virtually all advertising was in newspapers and magazines, *Printer's Ink* was a good name for a magazine directed to the advertising field. But today radio and television are just as important as print. So *Printer's Ink* is dead and *Advertising Age* reigns supreme.

One of the strongest publications in the world today is *The Wall Street Journal*. It has no real competitors. But *The Wall Street Journal* is a weak name for a daily business newspaper. The name implies a narrow, financial orientation. But the publication covers business generally.

Of such observations are opportunities fashioned.

Engineers and scientists in love with their own creations are responsible for some of the really bad names. Names like XD-12, for example. (Presumably standing for "experimental design number 12.") These are inside jokes that have no meaning in the mind of the prospect.

Take Mennen E, for example. People are literal and they take things literally. Mennen E deodorant was doomed to failure in spite of a $10 million advertising launch. The trouble was the name on the can. The introductory ad even admitted that the idea was a little unusual. "Vitamin E, incredibly, is a deodorant."

It is incredible. That is, unless they were appealing to people who want the strongest, best-fed, healthiest armpits in the country.

And what about Breck One and Colgate 100? Too many brand names today are meaningless.

With marginal differences in many product categories, a better name can mean millions of dollars of difference in sales.

"One" is the most overused word in the entire field of branding and a poor choice for any product. In addition to Pepsi One (which hasn't gone anywhere), there's Bank One, Channel One, CommerceOne, eOne, Fiber One, Global One, Mobil 1, Network One, OgilvyOne, One 2 One, One Health Plan, One.Tel, OneCoast, OnePoint, OneSoft, Oneworld, PureONE, Purina One, Radio One, Schwab OneSource, Source One, Square One, StratumOne, VerticalOne, V-ONE and Westwood One.

Nothing dramatizes meaningless names like today's dot.com crowd. Their names are almost impossible to remember.

When to Use a Meaningless Name

What about the obvious success of companies with coined meaningless names like Coca-Cola, Kodak and Xerox? What about them?

One of the things that makes positioning thinking difficult for many people is the failure to understand the role of timing.

The first company into the mind with a new product or new idea is going to become famous. Whether the name is Lindbergh, Smith or Rumplestiltskin.

Coca-Cola was first with a cola drink. Kodak with low-cost photography. Xerox with the plain-paper copier.

Take the word "Coke." Because of the success of Coca-Cola, the nickname Coke has acquired what the semanticists call secondary meanings.

Would you name a soft drink after the word for "the residue of coal burned in the absence of air"? Or the street name for the narcotic cocaine?

So strong is the secondary meaning of the word "Coke" that the Coca-Cola Company has nothing to fear from these negative connotations.

But choosing a coined, meaningless name like Keds, Kleenex or Kotex for a new product is dangerous, to say the least. Only when you are first in the mind with an absolutely new product that millions of people are certain to want can you afford the luxury of a mean-nothing name.

Then, of course, any name would work.

So stick with common descriptive words (Spray 'n Wash) and avoid the coined words (Qyx).

As a guide, the five most common initial letters are S, C, P, A and T. The five least common are X, Z, Y, Q and K. One out of eight English words starts with an S. One out of three thousand starts with an X.

This is still a very good positioning idea. "Margarine" has always been perceived as imitation butter. Since you can't change a mind once a mind is made up, a better strategy to overcome a negative is to change the name. "Soy butter" is real butter, only it's made from soy beans and not cow milk.

Negative Names Can Be Positive

Technology continues to create new and improved products. Yet they often are scarred at birth with second-class imitation names.

Take margarine, for example. Even though the product has been around for decades, it is still perceived as imitation butter. (It's not nice to fool Mother Nature.)

A better choice of name at the beginning would have helped. What should margarine have been called? Why "soy butter," of course.

The psychological problem with a name like "margarine" is that it is deceptive. It hides the origin of the product.

Everyone knows that butter is made from milk. But what's margarine made from? Because the origin of the product is hidden, the prospect assumes there must be something basically wrong with margarine.

Bringing the Product Out of the Closet

The first step in overcoming negative reactions is to bring the product out of the closet. To deliberately polarize the situation by using a negative name like soy butter.

That allows the development of a long-term program to sell the advantages of soy butter versus cow butter. An essential ingredient of such a program is "pride of origin" which the soy name connotes. (As does peanut butter, for that matter.)

The same principle is involved in the shift from colored to Negro to black.

"Negro" is a margarine name, forever relegating Negroes to second-class citizenship. "Colored" doesn't sufficiently polarize the situation. The implication is, the less colored the better.

"Black" is a much better choice. It allows the development of "pride of blackness," an essential first step to long-term equality. (You might prefer to be white, but I prefer to be black.)

In naming people or products, you should not let your competitors unfairly preempt words that you need to describe your own products. Like butter in the

Though a mouthful, "African American" has the advantage of shifting the focus from skin color to heritage. Another strategic improvement.

When you want to change a strongly held opinion, the first step to take is usually to change the name.

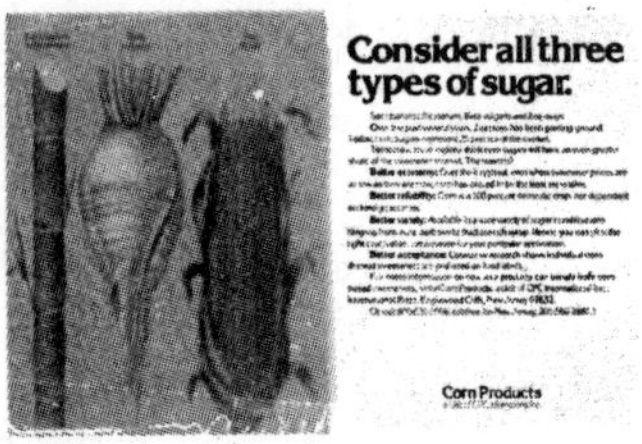

Here is the advertisement we ran for Corn Products. It represents a tactic you can use for almost any product that starts out with a negative perception. That is, find a way to level the playing field. And don't try to say you are better. Just say you are different. There are three types of sugar. Take your choice.

case of margarine. Or like sugar in the case of corn syrup.

A number of years ago, scientists found a way to make sweeteners out of corn starch. Result: products called dextrose, corn syrup and high-fructose corn syrup.

With names like "high-fructose corn syrup," it's no wonder that even in the trade the products were considered imitation or second-class in comparison with sucrose or "real sugar." So Corn Products, one of the major suppliers of corn syrups, decided to call its sweeteners "corn sugars." This move allowed the company to put corn on an equal footing with cane and beet.

"Consider all three types of sugar," say the ads. "Cane, beet and corn."

Marketing people should know that the Federal Trade Commission is the keeper of the generics for many industries. But the FTC can be persuaded. "If we can't call it sugar, can we put corn syrup in a soft drink and call the product 'sugar-free'?"

The extreme right of the political spectrum is on to this principle. The "Historic Preservation Association" is a fanatical foe of civil rights groups.

Special-interest groups recognize the power of a good name. The "Right to Life" movement and "fair trade" laws are two examples.

And what senator or representative would dare oppose a bill called the "Clean Air Act'?

In working against an established concept like "fair trade," it's important not to try to rename the competition. All you cause is confusion among your audience.

To counter the widespread consumer acceptance of

fair trade laws, the opposition tried to call it "price maintenance" legislation. It was many, many years before fair trade laws were repealed by the many states that had enacted them.

A better tactic is to turn the name around. That is, to reposition the concept by using the same words to turn the meaning inside out.

"Fair to the trade, but unfair to the consumer" is an example of this tactic.

Even better is to rename the opposition before the powerful name takes root. "Price maintenance" would probably have worked as a blocking strategy, but only early in the game. Another example of the importance of being first.

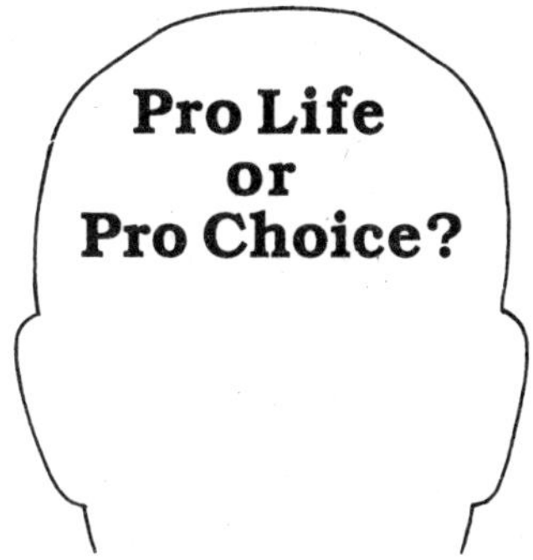

Each side of the abortion issue has selected positive words that put its position in the best possible light. The name you select for your "battle cry" is the most important and critical decision you will make. Give it a lot of thought.

David and Michael and Hubert and Elmer

In spite of the common belief that it's "only a name," there is a growing body of evidence that a person's name plays a significant role in the game of life.

Two psychology professors, Dr. Herbert Harari and Dr. John W. McDavid, were trying to find out why elementary-school students made fun of classmates with unusual names.

So they experimented with different names attributed to compositions supposedly written by fourth and fifth graders. Two sets of names, in particular, illustrate the principle.

There were two popular names (David and Michael) and two unpopular names (Hubert and Elmer) on some of the compositions. Each composition was given to a different group of elementary-school teachers to grade. (The teachers that participated in the experiment had no reason to believe they weren't grading ordinary school papers.)

Would you believe that compositions bearing the names of David and Michael averaged a letter grade higher than the same compositions attributed to Elmer and Hubert? "Teachers know from past experience," say the professors, "that a Hubert or an Elmer is generally a loser."

What about famous people with odd first names? Hubert Humphrey and Adlai Stevenson, for example. Both losers to men with the popular names of Richard and Dwight.

What if Richard Humphrey had run against Hubert Nixon? Would America have elected a Hubert Nixon?

Jimmy, Jerry, Richard, Lyndon, John, Dwight, Harry, Franklin. Not since Herbert have we had a "loser" name in the White House.

And who did Herbert Hoover beat in 1928? Another man with a loser name, Alfred.

In 1932, when Herbert ran against a "winner," Franklin, he lost. And he lost big.

What would you expect from someone named Edsel? Edsel was a loser name before Ford introduced the Edsel car. And the name contributed to the marketing disaster.

Take Cyril and John. According to psychologist David Sheppard, people wno don't know anyone with these names nevertheless expect a Cyril to be sneaky and a John to be trustworthy.

Ronald Reagan
Robert Redford
Marilyn Monroe

Alliteration is another good naming strategy because it makes a name more memorable. This is true for both brand names and personal names. It's interesting to note how many famous people have names that are alliterative.

You see what you expect to see. And a bad or inappropriate name sets up a chain reaction that only serves to confirm your initial unfavorable opinion.

Elmer is a loser. See, he's not doing that job very well. I told you, Elmer is a loser.

A true story. An account officer at a New York bank was named Young J. Boozer. Once when a customer asked to speak to "Young Boozer," he was told by the switchboard operator, "We have a lot of them around here. Which one do you want to talk to?"

We don't make these things up. We just report the facts. If your parents gave you the name "Young J. Boozer," what would you do? Most people we know would calmly accept their fate. "It's my name and I'm stuck with it." Don't be stupid; change your name. Would Marion Morrison have become the most famous movie star in history if he hadn't changed his name to John Wayne? We don't think so.

Hubert and Elmer in the Sky

The name is the first point of contact between the message and the mind.

It's not the goodness or badness of the name in an esthetic sense that determines the effectiveness of the message. It's the appropriateness of the name.

Take the airline industry, for example. The four largest domestic carriers are United Airlines, American Airlines, Trans World Airlines and . . .

Well, do you know the name of the "second largest passenger carrier of all the airlines in the free world," to use one of the airline's advertising slogans?

That's right. Eastern Airlines.

Like all airlines, Eastern has had its ups and downs. Unfortunately, more downs than ups. Among the four largest domestic airlines, Eastern consistently ranks fourth on passenger surveys.

Why? Eastern has a regional name that puts it in a different category in the prospect's mind than big nationwide names like American and United.

We ranted and raved about the Eastern name for 20 years until the company finally collapsed into Chapter 11 bankruptcy in March 1989. When Frank Borman (the former astronaut) was Eastern's president, he wrote us a letter admitting that the name is "somewhat provincial and has, in some cases, made it difficult to get national attention." However, he pointed out that "the name now has some 47 years behind it." A bad name doesn't get any better no matter how many years you have been using it.

The name Eastern puts the airline in the same category with Piedmont, Ozark and Southern.

You see what you expect to see. The passenger who has a bad experience on American or United says, "It was just one of those things." An exception to the good service he or she was expecting.

The passenger who has a bad experience on Eastern says, "It's that Eastern Airlines again." A continuation of the bad service he or she was expecting.

It's not that Eastern hasn't tried. A number of years ago, Eastern brought in some big-league marketing people and pulled out the throttle. Eastern was among the first to "paint the planes." "improve the food" and "dress up the flight attendants" in an effort to improve its reputation.

And Eastern hasn't been bashful when it comes to spending money. Year after year, it has one of the biggest advertising budgets in the industry. In a recent year, Eastern spent more than $20 million on advertising.

For all the money, what do you think of Eastern? Where do you think they fly? Up and down the East Coast, to New York, Boston, Philadelphia, Washington, Miami, right?

Well, Eastern also goes to St. Louis, New Orleans, Atlanta, Denver, Los Angeles, Acapulco, Mexico City.

Look at the problem from just one of Eastern's cities, Indianapolis. From Indianapolis, Eastern flies north to places like Chicago, Milwaukee and Minneapolis. And south to places like Louisville, Atlanta and Fort Lauderdale. They don't happen to fly east.

And then there is the lush San Juan run which Eastern has been serving for more than 30 years. Eastern used to get the lion's share of this market. Then American Airlines took over Trans Caribbean. So today, who is No. 1 to the San Juan sun? Why American, of course.

You can't hang "the wings of man" on a regional name. When prospects are given a choice, they are going to prefer the national airline, not the regional one.

The airline industry's problem is typical of the difficulty people have in separating reality from perception. Many experienced marketing people look at the Eastern situation in exactly the opposite way.

"It's not the name that gets Eastern into trouble," they say. "It's the poor service, the food, the baggage handling, the surly flight attendants." The perception is the reality.

What do you think of Piedmont Airlines? How about Ozark Airlines? And what about Allegheny? (In a survey of frequent travelers, 3 percent said they would avoid American and 3 percent United. But 26 percent said they would avoid Allegheny and 38 percent said they would avoid Eastern.)

Allegheny, of course, has thrown in the towel and become USAir. Even North Central and Southern gave up. In 1979 the two merged to become Republic Airlines. Now watch them take off.

In 1969, we made a presentation to Mohawk Airlines explaining why they should change their name. (Mohawk is a good name for a haircut, but not an airline.) In 1972, when Mohawk merged with Allegheny Airlines, we urged the surviving airline to change its name. "You're going to have to repaint half your fleet anyway," was one of our arguments, not to mention their nickname, "Agony Airlines." But no, they kept the Allegheny name. (Allegheny, Piedmont, Ozark: why were so many airlines named after mountain ranges?) In October 1979, they finally faced up to reality and changed the name to USAir. Today, US Airways is flying high, while Eastern is grounded. The arguments against this line of thinking are always the same. It's not the name, it's the product, the service, the price. That's not true at all. It's the perception of the product, the perception of the service, the perception of the price. Along with a bad name comes a bad perception.

The Akron Twins

Another common name problem is represented by two companies headquartered in Akron, Ohio.

What does a company do when its name (Good-

There are a lot of companies like B.F. Goodrich that need a name change. The question is, how do you change a corporate name? The worst way to do it is to hire an outside firm to develop a million-dollar name. That way, you get fanciful names like Agilent, Aventis, Navistar, Novartis. (Navistar recently went back to its original International name.) What you should generally do is to develop a product brand name that can eventually serve as a corporate name. For example, that's the strategy that B.F. Goodrich should follow. Introduce a fine brand that could eventually serve as a corporate name.

rich) is similar to the name of a larger company in the same field (Goodyear)?

Goodrich has problems. Research indicates that they could reinvent the wheel and Goodyear would get most of the credit.

Not surprisingly, B. F. Goodrich recognizes the problem. This is how they expressed it a number of years ago in an advertisement:

> The curse of Benjamin Franklin Goodrich. His name. It's one of fate's cruel accidents that our biggest competitor's name turns out to be almost identical to our founder's. Goodyear. Goodrich. Awfully confusing.

At the bottom of the ad, it says: "If you want Goodrich, you'll just have to remember Goodrich."

In other words, it's not Goodrich's problem at all. It's your problem.

B. F. Goodrich was the first domestic company to market steel-belted radial-ply tires in the United States. Yet several years later when tire buyers were asked which company makes steel-belted radials, 56 percent named Goodyear, which didn't make them for the domestic market. Only 47 percent said Goodrich, which did.

As they say in Akron, "Goodrich invents it. Firestone develops it. Goodyear sells it." In 1968 Goodyear had sales of $2.9 billion, while B. F. Goodrich's sales were $1.3 billion. A ratio of 2.2 to 1. Ten years later, in 1978, Goodyear had sales of $7.4 billion while B. F. Goodrich had sales of $2.5 billion. A ratio of 2.9 to 1. So the rich get richer. Fair enough.

But what is odd is that the loser's advertising continues to get all the publicity. "We're the other guys" got a lot of favorable attention in the press. But not a lot of favorable attention from the tire-buying public. Its name alone forever condemns Goodrich to eat the dust of its bigger competitor.

Goodrich is still eating dust.

The Toledo Triplets

If the Akron twins seem confusing, consider the predicament of the Toledo triplets. Owens-Illinois, Owens-Corning Fiberglas and Libbey-Owens-Ford.

These are not small outfits either. Owens-Illinois is a $2 billion company. Owens-Corning Fiberglas is a $1 billion company. And Libbey-Owens-Ford nearly a billion.

Look at the confusion problem from the point of view of Owens-Corning Fiberglas.

Owens, of course, is usually connected with Illinois. Owens-Illinois is a larger company with a stronger claim to the Owens name.

And Corning is usually linked with glass. In nearby Corning, New York, is the Corning Glass Works, also a billion-dollar company. It has succeeded in firmly linking the Corning name to the glass concept.

So what's left for Owens-Corning Fiberglas?

Fiberglas.

Which is probably why the company runs ads that say "Owens-Corning is Fiberglas." In other words, if you want Fiberglas, you'll just have to remember Owens-Corning.

OWENS CORNING

In 1992, Owens-Corning Fiberglas took our advice and changed its name. Unfortunately, they did the opposite of what we suggested. They dropped the "Fiberglas" and changed their name to "Owens Corning."

It would be a lot easier if the company changed its name to the Fiberglas Corporation. Then if you want fiberglass (with a lowercase "f"), all you have to remember is Fiberglas (with an uppercase "F"). This step would help focus the attention on the company's primary objective. To turn fiberglass from a generic back into a brand name.

The smoothest corporate name change in history was the change from Standard Oil of New Jersey to Exxon. Three factors were crucial: (1) The size of the company. Currently, Exxon is the fourth largest company in America and after its merger with Mobil, it should be the second largest. When you are a big company and you change your name, you get a lot of media attention. In other words, the media does your job for you. (2) The similarity of the Esso and Exxon names. The prospect was able to hook the two names together in the mind. (3) The street visibility of the new Exxon name. The thousands of gasoline stations that changed their name overnight made a strong impression in the minds of gasoline buyers.

What should you do if your name is Hubert or Elmer or Eastern or Goodrich or Owens-Corning Fiberglas? Change it.

But name changing is rare, in spite of the logic. Most companies are convinced they have too much equity in their present name. "Our customers and employees would never accept a new name."

What about Olin and Mobil and Uniroyal and Xerox? And how about Exxon Corporation? It was only a few years ago Exxon changed its name from . . .

Well, do you even remember what Exxon's old name was? No, it wasn't Esso and it wasn't Humble Oil or Enjay, although the company did use these names in its marketing operations.

The old name of Exxon Corporation was Standard Oil of New Jersey. Amazing what a few years and a few dollars can do.

There is only negative equity in a bad name. When the name is bad, things tend to get worse. When the name is good, things tend to get better.

Continental Confusion

Do you know the difference between a $3.9 billion company called The Continental Group, Inc., and a

$3.1 billion company called The Continental Corporation? Not too many people do until they find out that the Continental Group is the world's largest maker of cans and Continental Corporation is the big insurance company.

"Ah, yes. Continental Can and Continental Insurance. Now I know the companies you meant."

Why would a company drop "can" and "insurance" in favor of the anonymity of "group" and "corporation"? The obvious answer is that these two companies sell more than cans and insurance.

But is it possible to build an identity on a nothing name? Unlikely, especially when you consider the existence of other companies with claims on the Continental name. Especially Continental Airlines. And then there is Continental Oil, Continental Telephone and Continental Grain. Not to mention Continental Illinois Corp. (All billion-dollar companies, by the way.)

Both The Continental Group and The Continental Corporation are no longer independent companies. The Continental Group changed its name back to Continental Can and is now part of a dairy and packaging company, Suiza Foods. But they never learn. Recently Continental Grain changed its name to ContiGroup Companies.

Or how about the executive who says to his or her secretary, "Get me Continental on the phone."

It's not just "group" or "corporation" either. In Manhattan alone, there are 235 listings in the telephone directory starting with Continental.

The Too-Appropriate Name

Sometimes a name can be too appropriate. Too graphic, too suggestive. Especially in a product consumed in public.

Take the battle of the bulge. Mead Johnson's Metrecal versus Carnation's Slender.

This introduction of Diet Coke may turn out to be one of the most monumental marketing mistakes ever made. The Coca-Cola Company didn't need a new diet cola, they already had the leading diet cola brand, Tab. (The day Diet Coke was introduced, Tab was outselling Diet Pepsi by 32 percent.) By keeping NutraSweet out of the Tab product and putting it in Diet Coke only, they effectively killed the Tab brand. Today, however, Diet Coke is flat or declining in sales. (Mountain Dew has passed it to become the third largest selling soft drink after Coca-Cola Classic and Pepsi-Cola.) How long can a sugared product like Coke continue to dominate the soft-drink market? Who needs a "liquid refreshment" that contains no nutrients, no minerals and 150 empty calories? A transition from Coca-Cola to Tab would have been much easier than the one from Coke to Diet Coke because Tab doesn't carry the negative baggage of a diet name.

Even though Metrecal had the advantages of being first on the scene, the marketing victory went to Slender.

The choice of the name Slender, which connotes the benefit of using the product, was much more effective than Metrecal, a word invented by an IBM computer.

But when diet products are consumed in public, you have to be careful. No-Cal soft drinks were never a big success. Who wants to sit down in a restaurant and ask for a No-Cal cola? It's too easy to imagine what the people at the next table would think. "That fat slob."

How much nicer it is to ask for a Tab.

"With his inevitable glass of Tab in place," said *The New York Times* recently, "the president of New York University sat down to a business lunch."

Would he have ordered Diet-Rite Cola if he knew the press was going to be there?

When Lyndon Johnson was president, he had a special button on his intercom system for Fresca. And he didn't seem to care that everyone knew it.

Names for low-calorie and low-cost products have to be carefully selected to suggest the benefit without going over the line. If they become too blatant, they drive the prospect away.

10 The No-Name Trap

"I'm going to L.A.," the corporate executive will say. "And then I have to make a trip to New York." Why is Los Angeles often called L.A., but New York is seldom called N.Y.?

"I worked for GE for a couple of years and then went to Western Union." Why is General Electric often called GE, but Western Union is seldom called WU?

General Motors is often GM, American Motors is often AM, but Ford Motor is almost never FM.

Phonetic Shorthand

The principle at work here is phonetic shorthand.

Ra-di-o Cor-po-ra-tion of A-mer-i-ca is 12 syllables long. No wonder most people use R-C-A, three syllables long.

Gen-er-al E-lec-tric is six syllables long, so most people use G-E, two syllables.

Gen-er-al Mo-tors is often GM. A-mer-i-can Motors is often AM. But Ford Mo-tor is almost never referred to as FM. The single syllable Ford says it all.

But where there's no phonetic advantage, most people won't use initials. New York and N.Y. are both two syllables long. So while the initials N.Y. are often written, they are seldom spoken.

Los An-ge-les is four syllables long, so L.A. is frequently used. Note, too, that San Fran-cis-co, a four-syllable word, is seldom shortened to "S.F." Why? There's a perfectly good two-syllable word (Frisco) to use as shorthand for San Francisco. Which is why people say "Jer-sey" for New Jersey instead of "N.J."

When they have a choice of a word or a set of initials, both equal in phonetic length, people will invariably use the word, not the initials.

Phonetic length can sometimes fool you. The initials WU look a lot shorter than the name Western Union. But phonetically they are exactly the same length. Dou-ble-U U. West-ern Un-ion. (Except for W, every other English language letter is just one syllable.)

While customers refer to companies phonetically, the companies they talk about have a different way of looking at themselves. Companies are visually oriented. They go to a lot of trouble making sure the name looks right without considering how it sounds.

western union

One exception to the use of the initials WU instead of Western Union took place inside the corporation itself. For some reason, insiders consider it hip to use initials instead of names. So around the Western Union water coolers, you would hear not only WU, but also WUCO, pronounced "Woo-Coo," for Western Union Company. (We should know; we worked for the company for more than a decade.) Translating insider talk into language that outsiders can understand is one of the functions of a client's advertising and PR agencies.

Visual Shorthand

Business people also fall into the same trap. The first thing to go is the given name. When young Edmund

Gerald Brown starts up the executive ladder at General Manufacturing Corporation, he instantly becomes E. G. Brown from GMC on internal letters and memos.

But to be well known, avoid using initials. A fact known by most politicians. Which is why Governor Edmund Gerald Brown bills himself as Jerry Brown, not E. G. Brown. And E. M. Kennedy and J. E. Carter are billed as Ted Kennedy and Jimmy Carter.

What about FDR and JFK? The irony of the situation is that once you get to the top, once you are well known, then initials can be used without ambiguity. Franklin Delano Roosevelt and John Fitzgerald Kennedy could use initials only after they became famous. Not before.

The next thing to go is the name of the company. What starts out as visual shorthand to conserve paper and typing time ends up as the monogram of success.

IBM, AT&T, ITT, P&G, 3M. Sometimes it seems that membership in the Fortune 500 depends upon having a readily recognized set of initials. The moniker that tells the world you have made it.

So today we have such monikers as RCA, LTV, TRW, CPC, CBS, NCR, PPG, FMC, IC Industries, NL Industries, SCM, U.S. Industries, AMF, GAF, MCA, ACF, AMP, CF Industries, GATX, UV Industries, A-T-O, MAPCO, NVF, VF, DPF, EG&G and, would you believe, MBPXL.

These are not two-bit companies. All are currently on *Fortune*'s list of the 500 largest industrial companies. The smallest company on the list, EG&G, had

TIAA
CREF

Things always go from bad to worse. When we wrote this in 1980, there were 27 no-name companies on the Fortune 500 list. Today there are 44. Here's the complete list: AMP, AON, AT&T, BB&T, BJ's Wholesale Club, CBS, CHS Electronics, CMS Energy, CNF Transportation, CSX, CVS, DTE, EMC, FDX, FMC, FPL, GPU, GTE, IBP, IMC Global, ITT Industries, KN, LG&E Energy, LTV, Holding, TIAA-CREF, TJX, TRW, UAL, US Bancorp, U.S. Foodservice, USG, U.S. Industries, U.S. Office Products, USX and VF. (You have to admire a company that has the nerve to call itself TIAA-CREF. It's hard to see how TIAA-CREF is going to become a household word.)

Here's the list of 44 "name" companies on the current Fortune 500 list that are just below the "initial" companies. Don't these companies seem more familiar?

Ace Hardware
Allied Signal
Alltel
American Express
American Standard
Avery Dennison
Baltimore Gas & Electric
Bankamerica
Barnes & Noble
Campbell Soup
Central & South West
Consolidated Natural Gas
Consolidated Stores
Dana
Federated Department Stores
Gannett
Gateway
Harcourt General
Inacom
Kellogg
Kroger
Lear
Lehman Brothers
Masco
Merrill Lynch
Navistar International
Northeast Utilities
Owens-Illinois
Paccar
Phelps Dodge
Phillips Petroleum
Republic Industries
Safeco
Safeway
Sempra Energy
Shaw Industries
Sherwin-Williams
Tenet Healthcare
3Com
Transamerica
Tricon Global Restaurants
United Parcel Service
W.W. Grainger
Williams

sales of $375 million in a recent year and 13,900 employees.

If you select the next smaller company to every initial company on the Fortune 500 list, you will find the following: Rockwell International, Monsanto, National Steel, Raytheon, Owens-Illinois, United Brands, American Cyanamid, Reynolds Metals, H. J. Heinz, Interco, Hewlett-Packard, Carrier, Marmon, Polaroid, Diamond International, Blue Bell, Sperry & Hutchinson, Witco Chemical, Spencer Foods, Pabst Brewing, Cabot, Hart Schaffner & Marx, Cutler-Hammer, Gardner-Denver, Questor, Arvin Industries and Varian Associates.

Which list of companies are better known? The name companies, of course.

Some of the initial companies like RCA and CBS are well known, to be sure. But like FDR and JFK, these companies were well known before they dropped their names in favor of initials.

Which companies are likely to grow faster? Again, the name companies.

To test this point, we conducted a survey of both "name" and "initial" companies using a *Business Week* subscriber list. The results show the value of a name.

The average awareness of the "initial" companies was 49 percent. The average awareness of a matched group of "name" companies was 68 percent, 19 percentage points higher.

What drives big companies into committing corporate suicide? For one thing, the top executives have seen the company's initials on internal memos for so long they just naturally assume that everybody knows good old MBPXL. Then, too, they misread the reasons for the success of companies like IBM and GE.

No Shortcuts to Success

A company must be extremely well known before it can use initials successfully. Apparently the use of the initials "GE" triggers the words "General Electric" inside the brain.

Invariably, people must know the name first before they will respond to initials. The Federal Bureau of Investigation and the Internal Revenue Service are extremely well known. So we respond instantly to FBI and IRS.

But HUD is not recognized nearly so quickly. Why? Because most people don't know the Department of Housing and Urban Development. So if HUD wants to become better known, the department must first make the name Housing and Urban Development better known. Taking a shortcut by using only the initials HUD won't help very much.

Similarly, General Aniline & Film was not a very well-known company. When they changed their name to GAF, they made certain that they were never going to become very well known. Now that GAF has legally changed its name to initials, presumably there's no way to expose the prospect to the original name.

Yet alphabet soup seems to be on the corporate menu of many companies today. They fail to think through the process of positioning themselves in the mind. So they fall victim to the fad of the day.

When you see letters like GE, your mind thinks "General Electric." Try to think of a set of initials you remember (JFK, FDR, IBM, etc.) and see if you also can remember what those initials stand for. In general, if you remember the set of initials, you also remember the name. You can't make a set of initials famous unless you first make the name famous.

RCA

RCA as a company, of course, is no longer with us. It was bought by General Electric. Even if your initials stand for something in the short term, as RCA's initials did, you will generally weaken your company in the long term. We predict that many of the no-name companies mentioned in the preceding pages will gradually fade away, generally being bought out by their stronger competitors. Make no mistake about it. Initials make weak brand or company names.

And, no question about it, today's fad is "initialitus." Look at RCA. Everyone knows that RCA stands for Radio Corporation of America. So the company could use the initials to trigger the "Radio Corporation of America" words buried deep inside the mind.

But now that RCA is legally RCA, what will happen next? Nothing. At least in the next decade or so. The words are already buried in the minds of millions of people. And they'll stay there indefinitely.

But what about the next generation of prospects? What will they think when they see those strange initials, RCA?

Roman Catholic Archdiocese?

Positioning is like the game of life. A long-term proposition. Name decisions made today may not bear fruit until many, many years in the future.

The Mind Works by Ear

The primary reason name selection errors are so common is that executives live in an ocean of paper. Letters, memos, reports. Swimming in the Xerox sea, it's easy to forget that the mind works aurally. To utter a word, we first translate the letters into sounds. Which is why beginners move their lips when they read.

When you were a child, you first learned to speak and then to read. And you learned to read slowly and laboriously by saying the words out loud as you forced your mind to connect the written word with the aural sound stored in the brain.

By comparison, learning to speak requires much

less effort than learning to read. We store sounds directly and then play them back in various combinations as our mental dexterity improves.

As you grow up, you learn to translate written words into the aural language needed by the brain so rapidly that you are unaware the translation process is taking place.

Then you read in the paper that 80 percent of learning takes place through the eyes. Of course it does. But reading is only a portion of the learning process. Much learning occurs from visual clues which do not involve reading in the conventional sense at all. As when you learn the emotional state of another person by "reading" body clues.

When words are read, they are not understood until the visual/verbal translator in your brain takes over to make aural sense out of what you have seen.

In the same way, a musician learns to read music and hear the sound in his or her head, just as if someone were actually playing the tune on an instrument.

Try to memorize a poem without reading it out loud. It's far easier to memorize written material if we reinforce the aural component, the working language of the brain.

Which is why not only names, but also headlines, slogans and themes should be examined for their aural qualities. Even if you plan to use them in printed material only.

Did you think that Hubert and Elmer were bad names? If so, you must have translated the printed words into their aural equivalents. Because Hubert and Elmer don't look bad. They only sound bad.

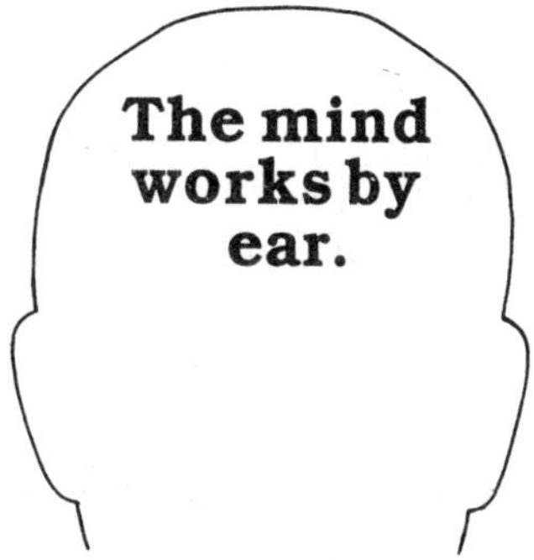

"The mind works by ear, not by eye." This is one of the most useful conceptual ideas in the entire book. Before you can file away a picture in the mind, you have to verbalize it. Every successful positioning program we studied was a verbally oriented program, not a visual one. (Think small, Avis is No. 2, etc.) It's not that pictures or illustrations weren't used, it's that the purpose of the visuals was to drive verbal ideas into the mind.

Many advertising agencies, on the other hand, still worship the visual. They love to create weird pictures that only cause visual distraction.

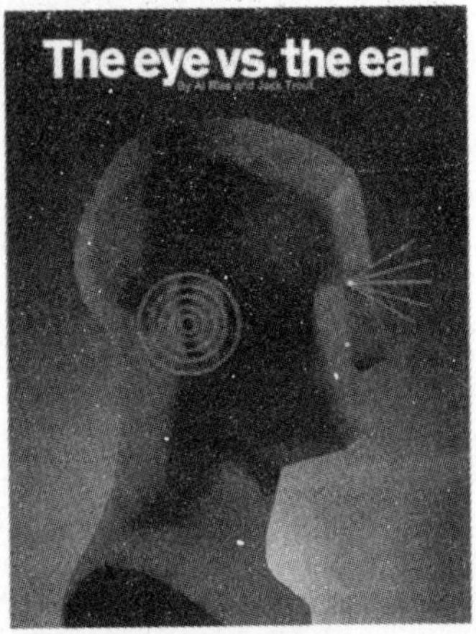

We went on to develop these ideas into a presentation called "The eye vs. the ear" for the Radio Advertising Bureau. Radio is truly the primary medium and "word of mouth" the primary communication vehicle. It's ironic that virtually the entire advertising industry today is visually oriented. "A picture is worth a thousand words" is the battle cry on Madison Avenue. (Which is why Coca-Cola uses polar bears, Budweiser uses lizards, Energizer uses the bunny.)

In a way, it's a shame that the print media (newspapers, magazines, outdoor advertising) came first and radio second. Radio is really the primal media. And print is the higher-level abstraction.

Messages would "sound better" in print if they were designed for radio first. Yet we usually do the reverse. We work first in print and then in the broadcast media.

Name Obsolescence

Another reason companies drop their names for initials is the obsolescence of the name itself. RCA sells a lot of things besides radios.

And how about United Shoe Machinery? The company had become a conglomerate. Furthermore, the domestic shoe machinery market was drying up as imports continually increased their share. What to do? They took the easy way out. United Shoe Machinery changed its name to USM Corporation. And lived anonymously ever after.

Smith-Corona-Marchant is another company which has lost its corporate identity. The result of mergers, Smith never did make coronas or marchants. So it decided to shorten the name to SCM Corporation.

Presumably, both SCM and USM made the change to escape the obsolete identity of the past. Yet the fact is that the exact opposite occurred.

The mind can't remember USM without dredging United Shoe Machinery from its subconscious.

At least RCA, USM and SCM had phonetic shorthand going for them. Without it, the difficulties are greater. Much, much greater. When Corn Products Company changed its name to CPC International, it found little recognition of the CPC name. The initials CPC are not phonetically shorter than Corn Products. Both are three syllables long, so the CPC initials were seldom used until the name change was made. Ask someone in the business if they are familiar with CPC International. See if they don't say, "Oh, you mean Corn Products Company?"

In our initial-happy society, the first question the mind normally asks itself is, "What do those initials stand for?"

The mind sees the letters AT&T and says, "Ah, American Telephone & Telegraph."

But what reply does the mind get when it sees TRW? Obviously, there are a fair number of people who remember the Thompson Ramo Wooldridge Corporation. And TRW is a $3 billion company, so it gets a lot of press and does a lot of advertising. But would those advertising dollars work harder if TRW had a "name" name instead of an initial name?

Some companies put sets of initials in series. How about trying to remember the D-M-E Corporation, a subsidiary of VSI Corporation?

We're not trying to suggest that companies shouldn't change their names. Quite the contrary. Nothing remains the same for very long. Times change. Products become obsolete. Markets come and go. And mergers are often necessary. So the time comes when a company must change its name.

U.S. Rubber was a worldwide corporation that marketed many products not made of rubber. Eaton

AT&T

As the years go by, the AT&T name gets weaker. The "telephone" part of the name is all right, but "telegraph" is now an obsolete word.

Yale & Towne was the result of a merger that produced a big company with a complicated name. Socony-Mobil was saddled with a first name that originally stood for Standard Oil Company of New York.

All of these names have been changed for sound marketing reasons. The traditional "foot-in-the-past" approach could have produced USR Corporation, EY&T Company and SM Inc. Three marketing monstrosities.

Instead, "forgetting the past" created three new modern corporate identities. Uniroyal, Eaton and Mobil. The marketing strengths of these names speak for themselves. These companies successfully forgot the past and positioned themselves against the future.

A company gets successful and then buys a Gulfstream V jet. You can't reverse the process and buy the jet first on the assumption that this is going to make you successful. If you make your name famous, you can then use your initials. But you can't reverse the process.

The Confusion Between Cause and Effect

In spite of the drawbacks, companies are lured to initials like moths to a candle. The success of the IBMs of this world seem to be proof that initials are effective. It's the classic confusion between cause and effect.

International Business Machines became so rich and famous (the cause) that everyone knew what company you were talking about when you used its initials (the effect).

When you try to reverse the procedure, it doesn't work. You can't use the initials of a company that is only modestly successful (the cause) and then expect it to become rich and famous (the effect).

It's like trying to become rich and famous by buying limousines and corporate jets. First, you have to become successful in order to have the money to buy the fringe benefits.

In some ways, the rush to adopt initials represents a desire to look accepted even at the cost of a loss in communications. In spite of all the publicity, many women think that ERA is a liquid detergent. Not the Equal Rights Amendment.

And look at the contrasting name strategies of two different airlines.

Pan A-mer-i-can Air-lines (seven syllables) has a phonetically long name. So they shortened it to Pan Am, two syllables. Much better than the initials PAA, which would be difficult to remember.

Trans World Air-lines (four syllables) is actually phonetically shorter than the T-Dou-ble-U-A they are using. But isn't TWA well known? Yes, it is, thanks to $30 million worth of advertising a year.

Although TWA spends more on advertising than its larger American and United competitors, surveys show that TWA has only about half the passenger preference of the other two. The inefficiency of the initials TWA is one reason.

What name should Trans World Airlines use?

"Trans World," of course. Only two syllables long, Trans World is short and graphic.

Acronyms and Phone Directories

Some companies get lucky. Their initials, either by design or by accident, form acronyms. For example: Fiat (Federation Internationale Automobiles Torino)

Since we wrote this, TWA has suffered greatly in the marketplace. (Last year the airline lost $353 million on revenues of $3.3 billion.) Its string of losses go back to 1988 when the airline saw its last annual profit. In 1992, TWA filed for bankruptcy. Building a brand on initials is like building a house on sand. "Wait a minute," our critics usually say. "It's the people, it's the service that really counts, not the name." How come the bad service always takes place on the airlines with the bad names?

and Sabena (Société Anonyme Belge d'Exploitation de la Navigation Aérienne).

Often organizations will select names that form acronyms with meaning. Two examples: CARE (Committee for Aid and Rehabilitation in Europe) and est (Erhardt Sensitivity Training).

Other companies aren't so lucky. When General Aniline & Film changed its name to GAF, it obviously forgot that the acronym sounds like "clumsy error." GAF is a gaffe in more ways than one.

The other thing people tend to forget when they pick a name is finding it in the telephone directory. Since you seldom look up your own name in a phone book, you might not realize how hard it is to locate.

Take USM Corporation, for example. In the Manhattan telephone directory, there are seven pages of listings starting with "US." So you ought to be able to find USM somewhere between US Lithograph and US Nature Products Corp.

But, of course, it's not there. Those US listings stand for "United States," as in the United States Lithograph Inc. The US in USM doesn't stand for anything. So following standard rules for alphabetizing, the phone company puts all initial names up front.

Generally speaking, it's a pretty depressing place. Look at a sample from the Rs: RHA Productions, RH Cleaners, RH Cosmetics, RH Cosmetics Corp., R&H Custom Upholstering, RH Garage, etc. As a matter of fact, there 27 listings starting with RH alone.

Fortunately, more and more companies are recognizing the dangers of the no-name trap. You can expect to see fewer and fewer MBPXLs.

SAP is another initial company with an unfortunate acronym. Sure, the company is currently successful because its enterprise resource planning software is a hot product in today's high-tech world. But in the long run, the name itself will tend to undermine the company's performance. Baan is another company in the same field with a similar problem. Neither of these names is as bad as Sappi, the world's largest producer of woodfree coated paper.

We were wrong. As we wrote earlier, alphabet soup names are alive and well.

11 The Free-Ride Trap

Take a product called Alka-Seltzer Plus. Let's see if we can visualize how Alka-Seltzer Plus might have gotten its name.

A bunch of the boys are sitting around a conference table trying to name a new cold remedy designed to compete with Dristan and Contac.

"I have it," says Harry. "Let's call it Alka-Seltzer Plus. That way we can take advantage of the $20 million a year we're already spending on the Alka-Seltzer name."

"Good thinking, Harry," and another money-saving idea is instantly accepted, as most money-saving ideas usually are.

But lo and behold, instead of eating into the Dristan and Contac market, the new product turns around and eats into the Alka-Seltzer market. .

Every so often the makers of Alka-Seltzer Plus redesign the bottle. The "Alka-Seltzer" gets smaller and smaller, and the "Plus" gets bigger and bigger.

A better name for the product would have been

Customers are easily confused. The initial reaction to Alka-Seltzer Plus was that it was an improved form of Alka-Seltzer rather than a new cold remedy. So the company made the Plus part of the name bigger. They should have given the brand a totally new name.

Bromo-Seltzer Plus. That way they could have taken business away from the competition.

The Conglomeration of the Corporation

In the product era life was simpler. Each company specialized in a single line. The name told it all.

Standard Oil, Singer, U.S. Steel, New York Central, Metro-Goldwyn-Mayer.

But technological progress created opportunities. So companies started branching into new fields.

Enter the conglomerate. The company that specializes in nothing. By development or acquisition, the conglomerate is prepared to enter any field in which it thinks it can make a buck.

Take General Electric. GE makes everything from jet engines to nuclear power plants to plastics.

RCA is in satellite communications, solid-state electronics and rent-a-cars.

Many people pooh-pooh the conglomerate. Companies should "stick to their knitting," they say. But conglomerates have provided the capital to sustain vigorous competition in the marketplace. If it weren't for the conglomerates, we would be a nation of semi-monopolies.

Take office copiers, for example. Xerox, the pioneer in the plain-paper field, now faces competition from a computer manufacturer (IBM), from a photo company (Kodak), from a mining company (3M), from a postage-meter company (Pitney-Bowes), from a mailing-list company (Addressograph-Multigraph).

Even when conglomerates grow by acquisition

XEROX

What happened in plain-paper copiers was a repeat of what happened in mainframe computers. After Xerox got into the mind first and established the premier position in copiers, a fistful of big companies jumped into the field: IBM, Kodak, 3M, Pitney-Bowes and Addressograph-Multigraph. None of these companies succeeded for the same reason that few of the dwarfs succeeded in the mainframe field. Their names conjured up the wrong positions in the mind. IBM means mainframe computers, Kodak means film photography, 3M means tape, Pitney-Bowes means postage meters and Addressograph-Multigraph used to mean printers. Why invent a new name when you can get a free ride on your existing name? Why indeed? So you can establish a new position in the mind.

(RCA's purchase of Hertz, ITT's purchase of Avis), they provide the money needed to sustain growth and competition.

Otherwise, when the original founders retired or died, the tax bite would leave the company too weak to defend its turf.

The typical life cycle of a corporation starts with an entrepreneur with an idea. If successful, you can count on two things, death and taxes, to ensure that the operation will end up as part of a conglomerate.

Two Different Strategies

Because companies grow by two different strategies (internal development or external acquisition), two different "name" strategies are evolving. Corporate egos dictate the strategies.

PricewaterhouseCoopers is our favorite ego name. No one loses face.

When a company develops a product internally, it usually puts the corporate name on the product. For example, General Electric computers.

When a company develops a product by external acquisition, it usually keeps the existing name. RCA kept the Hertz name. ITT kept the Avis name.

But not always.

Even today, Hertz and Avis are still powerful brands because they stand for a specific position in the mind, while the conglomerates that bought them (RCA and ITT) are weak brands. When you put your name on everything, you undermine your strength in the long term.

When Sperry-Rand developed a computer line internally, they called the product Univac. When Xerox went into computers by external acquisition, they changed the name from Scientific Data Systems to Xerox Data Systems.

Corporate egos aside, when should a company use the house name and when should they select a new name? (You can't really disregard corporate egos. Try telling General Electric not to put the GE name on a new product, and you'll begin to appreciate the enormity of the corporate ego problem.)

One reason why the principles of name selection remain so elusive is the Charles Lindbergh syndrome.

If you get into the mind first, any name is going to work.

If you didn't get there first, then you are flirting with disaster if you don't select an appropriate name.

International Business Machines was a bad name for a computer line, because IBM occupied the typewriter position in the prospect's mind.

But no matter. IBM was first in computers, so they made millions anyway. (Many, many millions.)

General Electric was also a bad name for a computer line. And furthermore they weren't first. So they lost millions.

Univac was a good name for a computer line, even though the present Sperry-Rand was very well known. So Univac continues to produce computer profits for Sperry-Rand.

And General Electric has long since gone from computers.

GENERAL ELECTRIC

How come General Electric is successful even though they seem to violate most of the principles in your book? This is probably the question we are asked most frequently. Actually there are a number of reasons. (1) GE is an 108-year-old company that got into minds when there was a lot less competition. (2) GE is the fifth largest company in America. Might often makes right. (3) GE focuses only on businesses where they can be No. 1 or No. 2. (4) For the most part, GE's competitors are also conglomerates with the same positioning liabilities that GE has. (5) GE avoids tomorrow-type businesses where the competition would kill them. Software, computers, telecommunications, networks, mobile phones, etc. Notice, too, they didn't change the National Broadcasting Company (NBC) to the GE Broadcasting Company (GBC). When your company is 108 years old, when your company is the fifth largest company in the United States, when your businesses are either No. 1 or No. 2 in their fields, when your company wants to give up on the future, by all means, use the General Electric strategy.

Divide and Conquer

To illustrate the advantages of separate names rather than house names, compare the strategies of Procter & Gamble with those of Colgate-Palmolive.

You'll find many house names in the Colgate-Palmolive line. To name a few: Colgate Dental Cream, Colgate Instant Shave, Colgate 100 Oral Antiseptic, Colgate Toothbrushes and Colgate Toothpowder. Also Palmolive Liquid Detergent, Palmolive Rapid Shave, Palmolive Shaving Cream and Palmolive Soap.

You won't find any house names in the Procter & Gamble lineup. (To consumers, Proctor, the iron, is as well known as Procter, the gamble.)

Procter & Gamble carefully positions each product so that it occupies a unique niche in the mind. For example: Tide makes clothes "white." Cheer makes them "whiter than white." And Bold makes them "bright."

What can we say? Procter & Gamble has pretty much given up on separate brands for separate products and has joined the line-extension crowd. (Their latest is the effort to extend the Oil of Olay brand into a general cosmetics brand.) Has Procter & Gamble done well lately? Of course not.

With fewer brands (51 major brands versus 65 for Colgate-Palmolive) Procter & Gamble does twice as much business and makes three times as much profit as Colgate-Palmolive.

While it's fashionable on Madison Avenue these days to pooh-pooh Procter & Gamble advertising, it's interesting to note that Procter & Gamble makes more money every year than all of America's 6,000 advertising agencies combined.

A New Product Needs a New Name

When a really new product comes along, it's almost always a mistake to hang a well-known name on it.

The reason is obvious. A well-known name got well known because it stood for something. It occupies a position in the prospect's mind. A really well-known name sits on the top rung of a sharply defined ladder.

The new product, if it's going to be successful, is

This Xerox computer advertisement nails the problem, but not the solution. Over the years, Xerox lost several billion dollars on their computer division until they finally threw in the towel and shifted their positioning efforts to "the document company." Everything that doesn't make a copy is pretty much gone.

going to require a new ladder. New ladder, new name. It's as simple as that.

Yet the pressures to go with the well-known name are enormous. "A well-known name has built-in acceptance. Our customers and prospects know us and our company, and they will be more likely to accept our new product if we have our name on it." The logic is overwhelming.

Yet history has destroyed this illusion.

Xerox spent almost a billion dollars for a profitable computer company with a perfectly good name, Scientific Data Systems. Then what did Xerox do? Of course. They changed the name of the company from Scientific Data Systems to Xerox Data Systems

Why? Obviously because Xerox was the better and more widely known name. And not only better known, but Xerox had a marketing mystique. A corporate Cinderella, Xerox could do no wrong.

The Teeter-Totter Principle

When you look into the prospect's mind, you can see what went wrong.

It's the teeter-totter principle. One name can't stand for two distinctly different products. When one goes up, the other goes down.

Xerox means copier, not computer. (If you asked your secretary to get you a Xerox copy, you'd be upset if you got a reel of mag tape.)

Even Xerox knew this.

"Funny. You don't look like a Xerox machine," said the headline of one of their computer ads.

"This Xerox machine can't make a copy," said another.

You knew that any Xerox machine that couldn't make a copy was headed for trouble. It was like a free ride on the Titanic. When Xerox folded its computer operations, it wrote off an additional $84.4 million.

What's a Heinz? It used to mean pickles. Heinz owned the pickle position and got the largest share.

Then the company made Heinz mean ketchup. Very successfully too. Heinz is now the No. 1 brand of ketchup.

But what happend to the other side of the teeter-totter? Why, of course, Heinz lost its pickle leadership to Vlasic.

To be successful, Xerox would have had to make Xerox mean computers. Does this make sense for a company that owns the copier position? A company that gets 90 percent of its volume from copiers?

Xerox is more than a name. It's a position. Like Kleenex, Hertz and Cadillac, Xerox represents a position of enormous long-term value.

It's bad enough when someone tries to take your position away. It's tragic when you do it to yourself.

Heinz is the bigger company with the better name, but Vlasic outsells Heinz in pickles and Gerber outsells Heinz in baby food. A big company with a big reputation usually cannot compete successfully with a smaller company with a well-defined position. Size doesn't matter. Positioning does.

Anonymity Is a Resource

One reason why companies keep looking for a free ride is that they underestimate the value of anonymity.

In politics, in marketing, in life, anonymity is a resource, easily squandered by too much publicity.

"You can't beat somebody with a nobody," goes the old political saying. But today you can.

The rapid rise of "nobody" John McCain illustrates the publicity advantages of anonymity. Steve Forbes, on the other hand, was well known for his 1996 campaign and therefore got much less favorable publicity in the year 2000. McCain lost, in our opinion, because he did not think through and refine his position. George Bush was the "compassionate conservative," but what was John McCain and what did he stand for? Being all things to everybody doesn't work in politics either.

The rapid rise of "nobody" Jimmy Carter in the midst of a host of somebodies is proof that politics is a different game today. The old maxims are no longer valid.

Richard Nixon may be the best-known political name in the world. But almost any nobody could beat him. The defeats of well-known political figures like Bella Abzug and Clifford Case are further proof that just being well known is no longer enough. You need a position.

A position that hopefully doesn't back you into the loser's corner. As age did to Senator Case and abrasiveness did to Ms. Abzug.

Publicity is like eating. Nothing kills the appetite quite as much as a hearty meal. And nothing kills the publicity potential of a product or a person quite as much as a cover story in a national magazine.

The media are constantly looking for the new and different, the fresh young face.

In dealing with media, you must conserve your anonymity until you are ready to spend it. And then when you spend it, spend it big. Always keeping in mind the objective is not publicity or communication for its own sake. But publicity to achieve a position in the prospect's mind.

An unknown company with an unknown product has much more to gain from publicity than a well-known company with an established product.

"In the future everyone will be famous for 15 minutes," Andy Warhol once predicted.

When your 15 minutes arrive, make the most of every 60 seconds.

12 The Line-Extension Trap

When the marketing history of the past decade is written, the single most significant trend will have to be line extension. That is, taking the name of an established product and using it on a new one. (The free-ride trap carried to its ultimate conclusion.)

Dial soap. Dial deodorant.

Life Savers candy. Life Savers gum.

Kleenex tissue. Kleenex towels.

Line extension has swept through the advertising and marketing community like Sherman through Georgia. And for some very sound reasons.

Logic is on the side of line extension. Arguments of economics. Trade acceptance. Consumer acceptance. Lower advertising costs. Increased income. The corporate image.

One of the loonier line extensions of recent years was Miller clear beer.

Inside-Out Thinking

As we said, logic is on the side of line extension. Truth, unfortunately, is not.

What's wrong with line extension? It's the net result of clear, hard-headed inside-out thinking that goes something like this:

"We make Dial soap, a great product that gets the biggest share of the bar-soap market. When our customers see Dial deodorant, they'll know it comes from the makers of the great Dial soap."

"Furthermore," and this is the clincher, "Dial is a deodorant soap. Our customers will expect us to produce a high-quality underarm deodorant." In short, Dial soap customers will buy Dial deodorants.

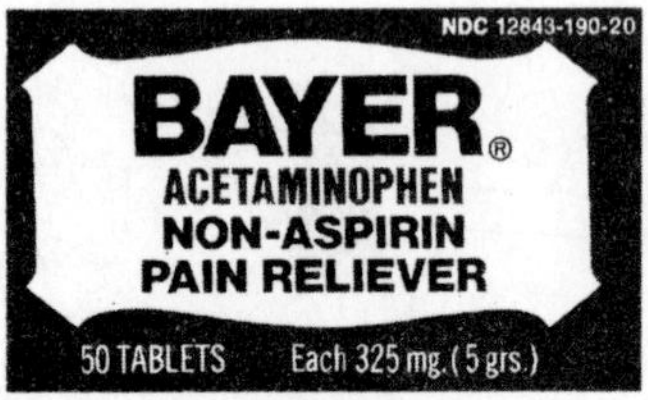

Grown men (we can't imagine women making this same mistake) sit around the conference table in the boardroom and decide to call their new acetaminophen product "Bayer non-aspirin." Will this brand take business away from Tylenol? Unlikely.

Notice, however, how the rationale changes when the line extension is in the same category.

Bayer "invented" aspirin and marketed the leading brand of analgesic for many years. But the people at Bayer couldn't fail to notice the progress made by the "anti-aspirin" approach used by Tylenol.

So Bayer introduced an acetaminophen product called "Bayer non-aspirin pain reliever." Presumably people who had been buying Tylenol and other acetaminophen products would now switch back to Bayer, the leading name in headache remedies.

But neither strategy worked.

Dial has a large share of the soap market and a very small share of the deodorant market.

And Bayer non-aspirin has only a tiny share of the acetaminophen market. A very tiny share.

Outside-In Thinking

Let's look at line extension from the point of view of the prospect and work backwards.

Both Dial and Bayer hold strong positions inside the prospect's mind.

But what does it mean to own a position in the mind? Simply this: the brand name becomes a surrogate or substitute for the generic name.

"Get me a Coke."

"Where is the Bayer?"

"Hand me the Dial."

The stronger the position, the more often this substitution takes place. Some brands are so strong they are practically generic. Fiberglas, Formica, Jello, Kleenex, Band-Aid, Sanka. "Generic" brand names are, of course, close to the edge, so they have to be handled carefully or Uncle Sam will take your goodies away.

From a communication point of view, the generic brand name is very efficient. One word serves in place of two. When you have a generic brand name, you can afford to ignore the brand and promote the category.

"Coffee keeps you awake? Drink Sanka brand." (You can see the heavy hand of the lawyers at work here. The theme would work better without the redundant word "brand.")

"Serve your family low-calorie Jello instead of cake or pie."

From the prospect's point of view, line extension works against the generic brand position. It blurs the sharp focus of the brand in the mind. No longer can the prospect say "Bayer" if he or she wants aspirin. Or "Dial" if one wants soap.

In a sense, line extension educates the prospect to the fact that Bayer is nothing but a brand name. It

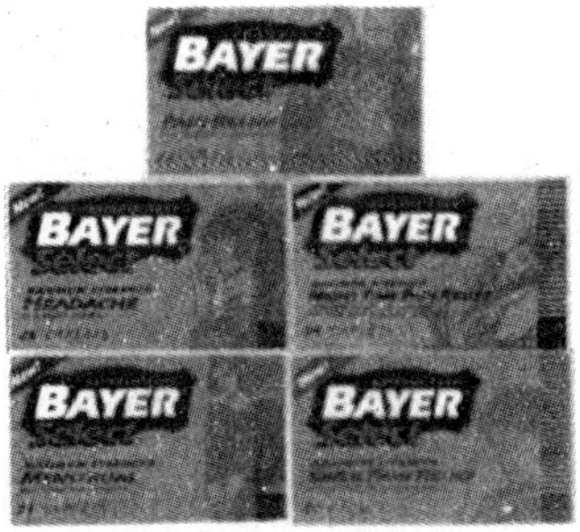

Bayer didn't give up. After the failure of the Bayer non-aspirin brand, they launched the Bayer Select line. Five different pain-relief products, none of which contains aspirin, all under the Bayer name. They spent $110 million launching the Bayer Select line. First year sales: $25 million.

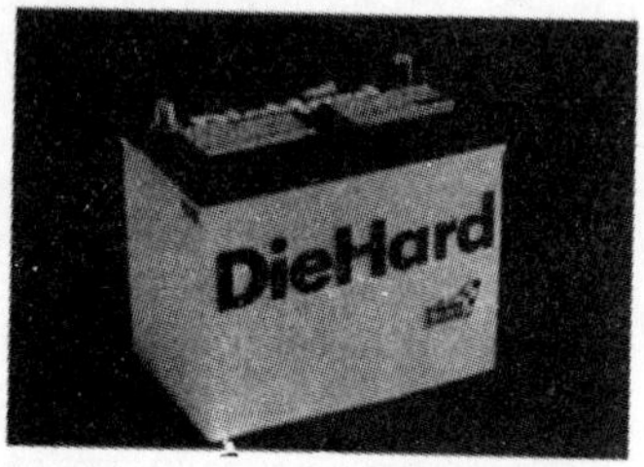

Sears was the largest retailer in the world when they introduced the DieHard battery. DieHard, of course, became the country's largest selling automobile battery. We're sure there were many voices inside Sears at the time saying, "Why not call it the Sears battery?"

destroys the illusion that Bayer is a superior form of aspirin. Or that Dial is deodorant soap rather than just a brand name for a deodorant soap.

JCPenney vs. DieHard

What actually gets driven into the mind is not the product at all but the "name" of the product which the prospect uses as a hook to hang attributes on.

So if the name of the automobile battery is the DieHard and Sears tells you that it will last 48 months, you have a hook (DieHard) to hang the long-lasting idea on.

But if the name of the battery is the JCPenney battery and the retailer tells you it never needs water, you have a very weak hook (JCPenney) to hang this feature on. (Not to mention the confusion between the company name and the product name.)

In a physical sense, the name is also like the point of a knife. It opens up the mind to let the message penetrate. With the right name, the product fills the creneau and stays there.

So why would JCPenney call it the JCPenney battery? Presumably there were other communicative words like DieHard available.

It's easy to see why if you apply "inside-out" thinking. "We're the JCPenney company. We're highly respected among all kinds of buyers including battery buyers. We'll put our own name on the product so that everyone will instantly know who made it and that it's an exceptionally good product."

Then the clincher. "With the JCPenney name on the battery, the prospect will know where to buy it."

"Terrific thinking, J. C." And another logical inside-out decision is made.

But when the tables are turned, the name makes no sense because the mind of the prospect is organized differently. The prospect thinks in terms of products.

It should come as no surprise that in terms of brand preference (the battery ladder in the mind of the prospect) the DieHard sits on the top rung and JCPenney is way down the line.

But doesn't a big retailer like JCPenney sell a lot of batteries? Of course, but as everyone knows, many products with the wrong name are sold "in spite of" rather than "because of."

On the other hand, doesn't the prospect have difficulty remembering that the DieHard battery can only be bought at Sears? Yes, it is a problem for Sears and not everyone who might want to buy the DieHard will be able to make the connection. But it's better to establish a position in the prospect's mind first and then worry about how to establish a retail connection later.

In positioning, the shortest distance between two points is not necessarily the best strategy. The obvious name isn't always the best name.

Inside-out thinking is the biggest barrier to success. Outside-in thinking is the biggest aid.

Two Ways of Looking at the Name

The consumer and the manufacturer see things in totally different ways.

Would you believe that to the folks down in Atlanta, Coca-Cola is not a soft drink? To the manufacturer, Coca-Cola is a company, a brand name, an institution and a great place to work.

But to the consumer, Coca-Cola is a sweet, dark, carbonated beverage. What's in the glass is Coke. It's not a cola drink manufactured by a company called Coca-Cola.

The tablets in a bottle of aspirin are Bayer. Not aspirin manufactured by a company called Bayer. (The company name, of course, is Sterling Drug, not Bayer. So Bayer non-aspirin could just as logically have been called Sterling non-aspirin.)

The great strength of a generic brand name is this close identification with the product itself. In the consumer's mind, Bayer is aspirin and every other aspirin brand becomes "imitation Bayer."

That famous Coca-Cola slogan, "The real thing," capitalizes on the tendency of the prospect to put the first product into the mind on a pedestal and to treat the me-too products as somehow inferior to the original.

If Coke or Kleenex or Bayer is not available or if other brands are cheap enough, then the prospect might buy something else. But Bayer would still own a strong position in the mind.

But notice what happens when the same customer is asked to buy a product called "Bayer non-aspirin." If Bayer is aspirin, how can Bayer also be non-aspirin?

Bayer timed-release aspirin, Bayer decongestant cold tablets, Bayer non-aspirin pain reliever. Each extension of the Bayer line undercuts the brand's aspirin position.

Marketing people know too much. They know that the name on the outside of the can is the brand name (and sometimes, too, the name of the manufacturer) of the stuff inside the can. It's a cola made by Coca-Cola. So why can't the company introduce a lemon-lime drink made by Coca-Cola instead of Sprite? They could, but prospects would find this deeply disturbing. To the cola drinker, Coca-Cola is the stuff inside the can. The brand name on the outside is just telling the drinker the name of the stuff on the inside. It's the real thing. You tinker with these perceptions at your own risk.

As you might expect, Bayer's total share of the analgesic market keeps falling.

What's a Protein 21?

Perhaps the classic example of the line extension trap is what happened to Protein 21 shampoo.

In 1970 the Mennen company introduced a combination shampoo/conditioner called Protein 21, which rapidly carved out a 13 percent share of the shampoo market.

Then Mennen hit the line extension lure. In rapid succession, the company introduced Protein 21 hairspray in regular and extra hold, scented and unscented. Also Protein 21 conditioner (in two formulas) and Protein 21 concentrate. And to make sure you can't remember what to put on your hair, Mennen also markets Protein 29. For men.

No wonder Protein 21's share of the shampoo market has fallen from 13 percent to 2 percent. And the decline is bound to continue.

But as incredible as it may seem, line extensions continue to sweep the packaged goods field.

The easiest way to kill a brand is to line-extend it. Protein 21 could be a big brand today if Mennen had not put the name on hairspray and conditioner products.

What's a Scott?

Take the position of Scott in paper products. Scott has the lion's share of the billion-dollar market for towels, napkins, toilet tissues and other consumer paper products. But Scott was weak where they thought they were strong.

Charmin	30 percent
Northern	14 percent
Scott	12 percent
Angel Soft	11 percent
Cottonelle	10 percent

Here are the current market shares for toilet tissue. Scott, once the leading brand, is now buried in third place. This is a bigger problem than it seems. When you lose your leadership, you don't just lose some business. You lose your power with the distribution, you lose your profit margins, you lose your reputation. Leadership alone is the most powerful position in marketing.

ScotTowels, ScotTissue, Scotties, Scotkins, even BabyScott diapers. All of these names undermined the Scott foundation. The more products hung on the Scott name, the less meaning the name had to the average consumer.

Take ScotTissue, for example. ScotTissue was the No. 1 brand in the toilet-tissue market. Then Mr. Whipple and his tissue squeezers at Procter & Gamble moved in. Now ScotTissue is second to Charmin, and you can expect the rest of the Scott line to cave in just as readily.

In Scott's case, a large share of market didn't mean they owned the position. More important is a large share of mind. The housewife could write "Charmin, Kleenex, Bounty and Pampers" on her shopping list and we'd know exactly what products she was going to get. "Scott" on a shopping list has no meaning.

The actual brand names aren't much help either. Which brand, for example, is engineered for the nose, Scotties or ScotTissue?

In positioning terms, the name Scott exists in limbo. It isn't firmly ensconced on any product ladder.

Scott has begun to see the error of its ways. Viva paper towels, a Scott brand, is a big winner. So is Cottonelle bathroom tissue.

What's a Life Saver?

Life Savers gum is another example of line extension that is going nowhere. Just hanging in there by the teeth, so to speak.

Again, the logic is on the side of line extension. In

an article in *The New York Times,* Life Savers' executive vice president explained the strategy:

"I am convinced that one way to improve the odds is by transferring an existing strong name to a new product requiring similar attributes."

Then he explains the attributes of Life Savers candy: "Our consumer dialogue indicates that the Life Savers brand name conveys more than merely the candy with the hole. It also means excellence in flavor, outstanding value and dependable quality."

Not exactly. How many people would have said "Life Savers" if you asked them, "What brand means excellence in flavor, outstanding value and dependable quality?" None.

Now what if you ask them "What's the name of the candy with the hole?"

Most people would say "Life Savers."

So what happened to the line extension? Life Savers gum never got more than a few percent of the market. One of those brands you won't see anymore because it was quietly killed in 1978.

As the television commercials used to say, "It's a great product, but where's the hole?"

The hole, of course, is not in the product at all. It's in the marketing strategy.

Ironically, Life Savers Inc. also has a big success in the gum field. The bubble gum field.

No, it wasn't Life Savers bubble gum.

It's Bubble Yum. The first brand of soft bubble gum. (The advantage of being first plus the advantage of not using a line-extension name.)

Bubble Yum is a runaway success. Sales already

We felt so strongly about the line-extension issue that we ran a full-page ad on the subject in the March 7, 1984 issue of *The New York Times.* "What is causing the decline of Miller High Life?" the ad asks, "It's the success of Miller Lite." History repeats itself. Coors Light just about killed regular Coors. And currently the success of Bud Light is causing a substantial decline in regular Budweiser sales. There's no such thing as a free launch.

exceed those of Life Savers candy. Not only is Bubble Yum the largest-selling brand of bubble gum, it's likely to become the largest-selling brand of chewing gum of any type.

What's an Eveready?

Many companies find themselves in rough water when new technologies rock their boats.

Eveready dominated the battery market when flashlights were the principal application. Then came the transistor and with it a host of new products including tape recorders and more powerful radios. And, of course, the longer-lasting alkaline batteries.

P. R. Mallory saw the opportunity and introduced the Duracell alkaline battery in a distinctive black and gold case.

The folks at Union Carbide pooh-poohed the idea of a new name. "We've already got the best name in the battery business," they said.

Not true. Today the Duracell outsells the Eveready alkaline power cell. To counter this successful strategy, the folks at Eveready apparently felt they had to copy Duracell's black and gold color scheme. And give the words "alkaline power cell" more prominence than the Eveready trademark.

The Duracell battery just says Duracell in bold type. It doesn't need to say "alkaline power cell" because Duracell means alkaline power cell.

This, of course, is the essence of positioning. To make your brand name stand for the generic. So the prospect freely uses the brand name for the generic.

Shortly after this book was published, we called up the Union Carbide advertising manager and told him that his company should introduce an alkaline battery with a new name. "We will never introduce a battery without the Eveready name," was his response. Enter the Energizer. (They had to introduce a new brand, Duracell was killing them.) Today, Duracell outsells Eveready and Energizer combined in spite of the fact that the public is enthralled with the Energizer bunny. (A contestant on the game show "21" lost $100,000 because he identified the bunny as belonging to Duracell.)

Yet line extension seems so intuitively right that the only way to resist the temptation is to study the classic line-extension mistakes of marketing history.

They're not hard to find. It's a saga of opportunities missed.

The 100 mm Dud

What's the name of the first extra-long, 100 mm cigarette?

Benson & Hedges, right? It's the best-known and largest-selling 100 mm brand.

"The disadvantages of Benson & Hedges" launched the brand and burned the name into the mind of the cigarette smokers. Benson & Hedges became known as the first, the original, the inventor of the 100 mm concept.

But, of course, it wasn't. The first 100 mm cigarette was Pall Mall Gold, but Pall Mall fell into the line-extension trap.

Then Benson & Hedges moved in and preempted the long-cigarette position

You'd think the missed opportunity represented by Pall Mall Gold would have discouraged them.

But it didn't. As we said, the logic in favor of line extension is overwhelming.

So now we have Pall Mall Menthol, Pall Mall Extra Mild and Pall Mall Light 100s. The confusion has detracted from sales of the basic Pall Mall brand.

Take Pall Mall Menthol, for example. Again, the logic is unassailable to the manufacturer. "Menthol cigarettes like Kool and Salem are getting a larger and

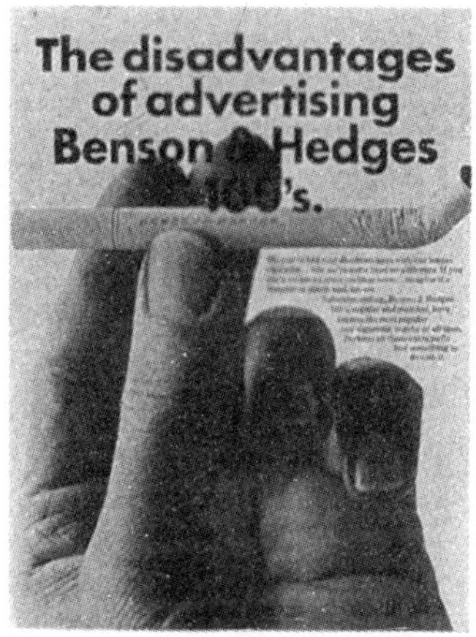

You don't have to be first in the marketplace to be a big winner. You have to be first in the mind. Pall Mall's line extension mistake allowed Benson & Hedges to get into the mind as the first 100mm cigarette.

larger share of the market. . . If we had a menthol brand, we could capture a share of that growing market."

Introducing Pall Mall Menthol. Which never achieved more than 7 percent of the volume of Kool.

In 1964 Pall Mall was the No. 1 cigarette brand in the United States.

In 1965 Pall Mall line-extended for the first time. They also fell to second place in sales. Every year since, Pall Mall's share of the American cigarette market has declined.

From 14.4 percent in 1964 to less than half that today.

The logic works two ways. Since regular brands represent a large share of the market, would you introduce a Kool nonmenthol?

Of course not. Kool was the original menthol cigarette. Kool means menthol. Like Bayer means aspirin.

It's a good thing for Kool, because most existing brands have become fair game for spin-off versions.

Today a well-stocked tobacco shop will carry well over 100 different brands (including line extensions). The industry produces in the neighborhood of 175 brands. It boggles the mind. (The smoke must affect the minds as well as the lungs of cigarette marketing people.)

Naturally, the two leading brands, Marlboro and Winston, have long since line-extended to lights, 100 mm and menthol. So according to the theory, can you expect to see the Marlboro and Winston brands follow

We should say a word about the success of Marlboro, the brand that became the largest selling cigarette in the world. Virtually all cigarette brands were making an effort to appeal to women. (Since most smokers were men, that's where the opportunity to expand the business seemed to lie.) Phillip Morris did just the opposite. They established the masculine position by focusing on a man's man, the cowboy. What's a Camel? Who knows? What's a Winston? Same answer. What's a Marlboro? A masculine cigarette that also happens to be the largest selling cigarette brand among women.

in Pall Mall's steps? Perhaps. But in the land of the blind, the one-eyed man is king.

What brands are left to challenge the leaders? Almost all major cigarette brands have been line-extended to death.

Perhaps what we need is a label for the maker as well as the smoker. "Warning: The marketing general has decided that line extension is dangerous to your profits."

Isn't Marlboro line-extended? Sure, but that's not the right question to ask. Would Phillip Morris be better off if the resources put into such extensions as Marlboro Menthol, Marlboro Mediums and Marlboro Milds were put into new brands? We think so, but then, again, we're opposed to cigarette smoking so we hope they don't take our advice. By the way, how many cowboys do you suppose smoke menthol cigarettes?

The Corn-Oil Comedown

Another missed opportunity happened in the margarine field.

Fleischmann's is the leading brand of corn-oil margarine and the biggest seller.

But the first corn-oil margarine was Mazola. A classic example of logic leading you astray.

Mazola was the name of the leading brand of liquid corn oil. What more logical choice for a corn-oil margarine than Mazola? Mazola corn oil. Mazola corn-oil margarine. And the rest is history.

Fleischmann's is the No. 1 brand today.

Oddly enough, Fleischmann's margarine, if you want to get technical, is a line-extended name. Remember Fleischmann's yeast? Fortunately for Fleischmann's, few people do because few people bake their own bread today.

And then there is Fleischmann's gin, vodka and whisky, also from the same company. The confusion factor is minimized because of the mental distance between a liquor product and a margarine. (Who really believes that Cadillac dog food is made by General Motors?)

The Coffee-Cup Caper

Another missed opportunity took place in the freeze-dried coffee field. Today Taster's Choice is the leading brand and the largest seller.

But what was the name of the first freeze-dried coffee? Maxim. So why isn't Maxim the No. 1 brand? It's a story of intrigue and courage that might be worth telling in more detail.

With its Maxwell House brand, General Foods owned the coffee market. The company got the largest share and made the most money. Then it invented a new process called "freeze-dried instant."

On the surface this seemed to be a way for General Foods to increase its share of the coffee market.

Or was it?

General Foods' opening move was good news for competition. By using the name Maxim, a spinoff of the Maxwell House name, the company instantly became vulnerable. (Maxim, Maxwell, get it? Most people didn't.) Maxim is a meaningless word that doesn't connote a benefit.

The Nestlé counterattack was named Taster's Choice. Not only was the strategic choice of the name superb, but Nestlé's timing was just about perfect. They jumped in as soon as possible, before the competitive Maxim name had a chance to penetrate the mind of the coffee buyer.

The untold story is the argument at Unilever about the name of their freeze-dried brand designed to compete with Maxim. Unilever management in Switzerland wanted to call the product "Nescafe Gold," to take advantage of Nescafe, the world's largest selling instant coffee. U.S. management, on the other hand, insisted on Taster's Choice and eventually won the internal as well as the external battle. A better name and a better strategy can sometimes overcome the disadvantage of being the second brand in the category.

The new name, Taster's Choice, also allowed them to attack ground-roasted coffee. "Tastes like ground roast," say the ads. Result? Well, you know the result.

Taster's Choice is the big winner in the coffee-cup caper. In spite of the fact that General Foods invented the freeze-dried category and was first on the scene, Taster's Choice outsells Maxim more than two to one.

The Fickle-Fingers Affair

Another missed opportunity is known in hand lotion circles as "the fickle fingers affair." The story starts with Jergens, the No. 1 brand with the dominant share of market.

First, the company introduced Jergens Extra Dry, a cream-like product in an era of liquid-like lotions. Jergens Extra Dry was really a significant innovation smothered by the similarity of names. The prospect didn't recognize the difference.

But the competition did.

Chesebrough-Pond's introduced Intensive Care. Now for the first time, the new cream-like lotion had a name which positioned the product clearly in the consumer's mind. And the product took off.

Of course, when Jergens realized what was happening, they countered with a brand called Direct Aid.

But it was the old story of too little and too late because the marketing victory went to Intensive Care. Today Intensive Care is the No. 1 brand. It outsells Jergens, Jergens Extra Dry and Direct Aid combined.

But isn't the brand really called "Vaseline Intensive Care," a line-extended name?

One of the most important positioning ideas is demonstrated by the success of Intensive Care. A line extension introduced by a competitor often represents an opportunity for your company. Jump on the line extension with a different name and the battle will generally go your way. Benson & Hedges, Taster's Choice and Intensive Care are three typical examples.

True, but customers call the product Intensive Care, not Vaseline. Vaseline is petroleum jelly. Intensive Care is a hand lotion.

When you believe in line extension, you never let the facts get in the way of your beliefs. In spite of the fact that Tab outsold Diet Pepsi, thereby confirming the inferiority of a line-extension name, Pepsi-Cola went on their merry, line-extension way introducing such products as Crystal Pepsi, Wild Cherry Pepsi, Pepsi Max, and Pepsi XL. There's also Pepsi Light, Pepsi AM, Pepsi Max and Pepsi One. None of these brands have gone or will go anywhere.

The Diet-Cola War

Very seldom does one get a chance to observe a direct confrontation between two products with such diametrically opposed strategies as the conflict betwen Diet Pepsi and Tab.

What makes line extension so insidious is that all the advantages seemed to be on the Pepsi side of the counter. After all, a well-known name like Pepsi combined with the descriptive adjective "Diet" would seem to be invincible.

Furthermore, Diet Pepsi was the first on the scene. According to the rules of positioning, the brand that gets into the mind of the prospect first has an enormous advantage. But not enough to overcome the disadvantages of a line-extended name.

The marketing winner is Tab. The line extension of the Pepsi name into the diet cola field is not a strength. It's a weakness.

The cola drinker sees Diet Pepsi as an inferior product to regular Pepsi, while Tab stands on its own.

So with the brilliant Tab marketing success, did the Coca-Cola Company abide by the principles of positioning?

Why, of course not. They proceeded to make the same mistake. Tab now also comes in root beer, ginger ale and black cherry. If they wanted to build brands in these categories, they should not have used the brand name which has become the generic "diet cola" name.

And what about the loser? There's nothing like the loss of a key ballgame to get the coach to change the strategy. So what happened at Pepsi Cola?

They made the same mistake again. Enter Pepsi Light. A lightweight line-extension name.

Today's Light is Pepsi One. They can't stop fooling around.

Reverse Line Extension

While line extension is usually a mistake, the reverse can work. Reverse line extension is called "broadening the base." One of the best examples is Johnson's baby shampoo.

By promoting the mildness of the product to the adult market, the company has made Johnson's baby shampoo one of the leading brands of adult shampoo.

Notice the characteristics of this broadening-the-base strategy. Same product, same package, same label. Only the application has changed.

If Johnson & Johnson had line-extended the product and introduced Johnson's adult shampoo, the product would not have been nearly as successful.

Other examples of broadening the base include Blue Nun, a white wine being promoted as equally good with meat courses as with fish.

But aren't these examples of the "everybody trap?" Not exactly. Johnson's baby shampoo is the first and only baby shampoo being promoted as an adult product too. And Blue Nun is the only white wine being promoted as good with meat as well as fish.

If other brands tried the same approach, they wouldn't be nearly as successful as these two.

Johnson's Baby Shampoo actually became the leading adult shampoo for a short period of time. Then Johnson & Johnson backed off its advertising program and let the brand drift. Some products need heavy levels of advertising to keep the idea of the brand alive in the mind. This strategy doesn't necessarily increase sales, rather it maintains them at existing levels. Too many companies, however, try to measure advertising on a "return on investment" basis.

Arm & Hammer has extended its brand name to a wide variety of products—toothpaste, carpet cleaner, etc. Most of these products were modest successes at best. The question is, how much better off would the company have been if it had used some of its technological skills to introduce new categories with new names? Mentadent, a toothpaste with a baking soda ingredient, outsells Arm & Hammer toothpaste. Falling in love with your brand name is a common occurrence in Corporate America.

Even *The Harvard Business Review* has come out and declared that line extension was a no-no. Why won't anyone listen.

And then there is Arm & Hammer baking soda, being promoted as good for refrigerators and drains. Very successfully too. But what happened when the same company line-extended with Arm & Hammer, the baking soda deodorant?

Very little. As Phyllis Diller says, "It only works if you're standing in the refrigerator."

13 When Line Extension Can Work

Line extension is popular. No doubt about it.

In New York City the professional baseball, football, basketball and tennis teams are known as the Mets, Jets, Nets and Sets.

The city's off-track betting offices have put up posters featuring the New York Bets. If the city had a gym team, presumably they would be called the New York Sweats.

Why stop there? A street gang could be the New York Ghetts. City planners, the New York Debts.

Fortunately for one's sanity, the trend seems to be in the other direction. The tennis team has seen the light and has changed its name from the New York Sets to the New York Apples.

Short-Term Advantages

One of the reasons for the continuing popularity of line extension is that in the short term, line extension has some advantages.

Let's say there was going to be a professional swimming team in New York. "Here come the Wets" might be a typical newspaper headline announcing the event. With one word, "Wets," we know it's (1) a professional sports team, (2) located in the metropolitan New York area and (3) involved in some kind of water sport.

But that's only in the short term. As the original announcement fades in the mind, confusion sets in.

Is there really a swimming team called the Wets? Or have I confused them with a basketball team called the Nets? Or was I thinking about a tennis team called the Sets? Now let's see, the Nets changed their name to the Apples. Or was it the Sets?

Because the line-extension name is related to the original name, it achieves an instant flash of understanding. "Ah, yes, Diet Coca-Cola."

It also generates an instant flash of sales. When Alka-Seltzer announces a new product like Alka-Seltzer Plus, everybody stocks up on it. Consumers aren't necessarily buying it, but retailers are.

So the early sales figures look good. (To book a million dollars' worth of business, you only have to sell five dollars' worth to every supermarket.)

Business looks great the first six months as you fill the pipelines. But when the reorders don't come in, all of a sudden things turn dark.

One of the keys to understanding the line-extension issue is to separate the short-term effects from the long-term effects. Is alcohol a stimulant or a depressant? Actually, it's both. In the short term alcohol is a stimulant; in the long term alcohol is a depressant. Line extensions generally work the same way.

Long-Term Disadvantages

After the initial recognition of a line-extension brand, the prospect is never quite sure there is such a product.

Schlitz Light, Pall Mall Extra Mild, Jergens Extra Dry. Brand names like these slide into (and out of) the mind effortlessly. They require almost no mental work on the part of the prospect.

Easy come, easy go. Line-extension names are forgettable because they have no independent position in the mind. They are satellites to the original brand name. Their only contribution is to blur the position occupied by the original name. Often with catastrophic results.

Way back in the thirties, the Ralston Purina Company was running radio commercials for "Ralston 1, 2, 3." One was Shredded Ralston. Two was Regular Ralston. Three was Instant Ralston.

One, two, three, gone.

And the legendary David Ogilvy broke his pencil on Rinso White/Rinso Blue.

Sara Lee tried to get into the frozen dinner field with products like Sara Lee Chicken & Noodles Au Gratin. Sara Lee owns the dessert position. Nobody doesn't like Sara Lee, but there were a lot of people out there who didn't like the chicken & noodles au gratin. And didn't buy it. Especially with the name Sara Lee on it.

So the kitchens of Sara Lee came in out of the frozen entree field. After dropping some $8 million on the project.

Almost everybody has tried line extension. *Saturday Review Magazine* tried to publish in four different flavors. (*The Arts, Science, Education, The Society*.) A $17 million loss.

Currently, Levi Strauss and Brown Shoe are

The list of failed line extensions is exceptionally long. USA Today on TV lost $15 million in its first year and was canceled in its second. Notice, however, that media reports of its demise never mentioned the line-extension angle. It's always the program, the talent, the timing, the set, etc. This is the essential "product vs. positioning" issue. We believe that the right name and the right positioning can make a success out of products or services that are, at best, average. Most people believe that the only thing that counts is the quality of the product or service itself. Not true.

Levi Strauss first tried to introduce a product called "Levi's Tailored Classics," which didn't go anywhere. Then they took essentially the same product and renamed it Dockers. Today Dockers is a worldwide brand that does $1.5 billion in business. Their shoe line "Levi's for Feet" died a quick death.

launching, would you believe, "Levi's for Feet." Levi is, by far, the market leader in jeans, but this time they booted it.

Then there is Avis flowers, Zenith watches, Old Grand-Dad tobacco, Bic pantyhose, Kleenex diapers.

And then there is Pierre Cardin wine. In both red and white, of course. And Chanel for Men. Which leads one to ask, "Will Burt Reynolds replace Catherine Deneuve?"

"Two" seems to be a popular line-extension concept. We have Alka-2, Dial 2, Sominex 2, as well as Jaws 2. (Almost never has a motion picture sequel generated as much business as the original.)

Even supposedly sophisticated advertising agencies have jumped into twos. So now we have Ogilvy & Mather 2, Doyle Dane Bernbach 2, N. W. Ayer 2 and Grey 2, to name a few twos.

The Shopping-List Test

The classic test for line extension is the shopping list.

Just list the brands you want to buy on a piece of paper and send your spouse to the supermarket: Kleenex, Crest, Listerine, Life Savers, Bayer and Dial.

That's easy enough. Most husbands or wives would come back with Kleenex tissue, Crest toothpaste, Listerine mouthwash, Life Savers candy, Bayer aspirin and Dial soap.

Line extensions like Kleenex towels, Life Savers gum, Bayer non-aspirin and Dial antiperspirants have not destroyed the brands' original positions. Yet. But give them enough time to hang themselves.

How about this list: Heinz, Scott, Protein 21, Kraft.

Will your spouse bring back Heinz pickles or ketchup (or perhaps baby food)? Scott tissue or towels? Protein 21 shampoo, hairspray or conditioner? Kraft cheese, mayonnaise or salad dressing?

The confusion caused when one name stands for more than one product is slowly but surely sapping the strength of brands like Scott and Kraft.

Like a star that's overexpanded, the brand eventually becomes a burned-out hulk. An enormous marketing white elephant. What makes line extension so insidious is that the disease takes many years to exact its toll. Many years of slow, debilitating existence.

Take Kraft. A famous name which suffers from terminal line extension.

What's a Kraft? It's everything and yet it's nothing. In almost no categories is the Kraft brand number one. In mayonnaise, Kraft is second to Hellmann's. In salad dressing, Kraft is second to Wishbone.

Where Kraftco has the leading brand in a category, they don't call it Kraft.

In cream cheese, it's Philadelphia, not Kraft.

In ice cream, it's Sealtest, not Kraft.

In margarine, it's Parkay, not Kraft.

Where is the strength of the Kraft name? It's too diffuse. Kraft means everything and nothing. Line extension is a weakness, not a strength.

What about cheese? Surely Kraft is a strong name in cheese. And it is.

"America," say the ads, "spells cheese K-R-A-F-T." Terrible spelling and terrible strategy.

KRAFT

Maybe we were a little too hard on the Kraft brand. It's a brand like General Electric that has been around forever. Fine for cheese, but not necessarily powerful in other categories. If we were Kraft, we would focus on new brands for new categories.

Marketing is like horse racing. The winning horse is not necessarily a good horse. It all depends on the ability of the horses in the race. In a claiming race, the winner is the best of the worst. In a stakes race, the best of the best.

Kraft has been successful in cheese. Now, name all of the other cheese brands you know.

Kraft is a winner in a claiming race.

Where there are no brands or weak brands, you can line-extend. But as soon as strong competition arrives, you're in trouble.

Tanqueray made a big splash when they tried to introduce a vodka to go along with their well-known gin brand. Is Tanqueray vodka going to take business from Absolut and Stolichnaya? Absolutely not.

The Bartender Test

In addition to the shopping list test, there's the bartender test. What do you get when you order the brand by name?

"J&B on the rocks" should get you scotch. "A Beefeater martini" should arrive with gin. And "a bottle of Dom Perignon" will definitely get you champagne.

What about "Cutty on the rocks"? You'll get scotch, of course, but will you get Cutty Sark or the more expensive 12-year-old Cutty 12?

Cutty 12 is the Diet Pepsi of the scotch category. A well-known name (Cutty) combined with a descriptive adjective (12). Very logical from the point of view of the distillery. But what about the point of view of the drinker?

When you order "Chivas on the rocks," you let everyone know you want the best. Chivas Regal.

To get Cutty 12, you can't just say "Cutty." And when you add the "12," you're never quite sure whether the bartender heard you or, just as important, whether the people around you heard the "12."

Nor does the promotion of Cutty 12 help the original Cutty Sark brand. It's a constant reminder to the Cutty Sark drinker that he or she is drinking a lower-quality product.

Cutty 12 got into the ballgame after Chivas Regal, so we shouldn't have expected much. But there was a 12-year-old brand of scotch in the U.S. market well before Chivas.

Johnnie Walker Black Label.

Today, of course, Chivas Regal outsells Johnnie Walker Black Label about two to one.

"Give me a Johnnie Walker with a splash, bartender."

"Black Label or Red Label, sir?"

"Aaaaaaaaaaah . . . the hell with it. Make it a Chivas."

Cutty 12 and Johnnie Walker Black Label are step-up examples of line extension. They usually result in anemic sales at the higher-priced end. (Who wants to pay premium prices for a low-price name?)

No brand will live forever. There's a fashion element in many products such as clothing and liquor. The hot brands used to be "brown" goods, whisky or scotch. Today the hot brands are "white" goods like vodka and tequila. It wouldn't surprise us at all to see tequila outsell vodka somewhere down the road. Can we expect to see an Absolut tequila? Absolutely.

What's a Packard?

The step-down problem is just the reverse. Step-down products are often instantly successful. The hangover comes later.

Before World War II Packard was the premier American automobile. More so even than Cadillac, it was a status symbol esteemed all over the world.

Heads of state bought armored Packards. One was

made for Franklin Roosevelt. Like Rolls-Royce, Packard loftily declined the annual model-change policy of lesser makers.

Then in the middle thirties, Packard introduced their first step-down model, the relatively inexpensive Packard Clipper.

The Packard Clipper was the most successful car Packard ever built. Sales were terrific, but it killed the company. (Or more precisely, it killed Packard's prestige position, which in turn killed the company.)

Packard drifted along until 1954 when Studebaker absorbed the company. The end of the road came four years later.

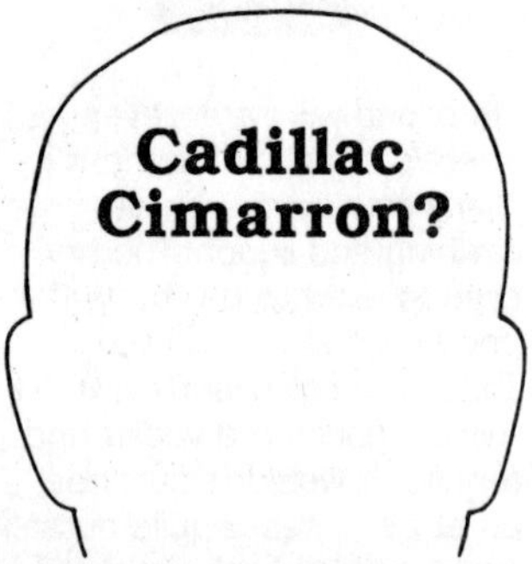

We were wrong about the Cadillac Seville. It's still with us. Maybe it wasn't as small as we thought. But the next Cadillac venture into the small car arena, the Cadillac Cimarron, was a failure. But they didn't give up. They came back with the Catera, the "Caddy that zigs." No small Cadillac is ever going to be a big deal on the road, because it conflicts with what's inside the prospect's mind. Cadillacs have the perception of being big cars.

What's a Cadillac?

What do you know about Cadillac? How long is it? What colors does it come in? What's the horsepower of the engine? What options are available?

To the average automobile prospect, General Motors has succeeded in communicating almost nothing about Cadillac. Except its position as the top-of-the-line, domestic luxury automobile.

But even General Motors sometimes forgets that for every product there are two points of view. And most line-extension mistakes are made because the marketer did not appreciate this fact.

What's a Cadillac? This might surprise you, but from General Motors' point of view, a Cadillac is not an automobile at all. It's a division. As a matter of fact, it's one of GM's most profitable divisions

But from the buyer's point of view, Cadillac is a big luxury car. You can see the problem.

Because of the gasoline situation, Cadillac is worried. So to maintain that profitability, General Motors has introduced a small Cadillac, the Seville.

Cadillacs that look like Chevrolets will always be losers.

Short-term, Cadillac will sell a lot of Sevilles. But long-term a mini-Cadillac conflicts with the big-car position that Cadillac owns in the mind.

So the prospect looks at the Seville and asks, "Is it or isn't it a Cadillac?"

Long-term, the Seville gets in the way of the most effective answer to the Mercedes challenge. A separate high-price name and a separate dealer organization.

What's a Chevrolet?

For automobiles as well as other products, you can ask yourself that age-old question and you'll know if you have a positioning problem.

What is it?

For example, what's a Chevrolet? It's a car that's fallen into the everybody trap. By trying to appeal to everybody, a product winds up appealing to nobody.

What's a Chevrolet? We'll tell you what a Chevrolet is. It's a big, small, cheap, expensive car.

O.K., how come Chevy is still No. 1? How come they haven't lost their leadership to Ford?

To which we reply, "What's a Ford?" Same problem. Ford is also a big, small, cheap, expensive car.

Ford has another problem. Not only is Ford an automobile. Ford is also a company and a person.

Chevrolet did lose their leadership to Ford. And, in our opinion, for the reason stated in the text. They tried to be all things to everybody. Over the past two decades, Chevrolet has constantly marketed a broader range of automobiles than Ford. Currently, for example, Chevrolet has 9 car models and Ford has only 7. But it's more than just the number of models. Ford has had more of a focus on its Taurus model. What's the focus of the Chevrolet line? Who knows?

A Ford might be all right, but there is a real problem in selling Ford Mercurys or Ford Lincolns. (One reason why the Ford Motor Company has always had a hard time selling higher-priced cars.)

What's a Volkswagen?

The rise and fall and rise of Volkswagen is one of the most remarkable stories of the power of perception. Volkswagen was the first automobile to capture the small car position in the mind. Then they thought big and sales collapsed. Then they thought small again and sales took off. Lesson: Don't try to change a human mind.

A line-extension tragedy usually moves to its inevitable conclusion in three acts.

Act One is the big success, the big breakthrough. Usually the result of finding a wide-open creneau and then exploiting it brilliantly.

Volkswagen invented the small-car position and moved rapidly to exploit the breakthrough. "Think small," perhaps the most famous single advertisement ever run, stated the position in no uncertain terms.

Very quickly, the Volkswagen Beetle established an exceptionally strong position in the automotive market. Like most classic success stories, Volkswagen became more than a brand name for a product.

"I drive a Volkswagen" says more than who made the automobile the person owns. "I drive a Volkswagen" says something about the owner's way of life. A no-nonsense, practical person, self-confident about his or her status in life. A simple, functional piece of transportation equipment.

The Volkswagen owner is a reverse snob. He or she loves to put down the car buyer who loves to impress the neighbors. "The 1970 Volkswagen will stay ugly longer" expresses this attitude perfectly.

Act Two is fueled by greed and visions of unending successes. So Volkswagen extends Volkswagen reliability and quality to bigger, more expensive cars. To buses and "Jeeps."

The ultimate is the Dasher. "With great pride, Volkswagen enters the luxury car field," say the announcement ads.

"Dasher. The elegant Volkswagen."

The elegant Volkswagen? "A striking interior. Rich appointments," say the ads. This is a Volkswagen? What happened to that no-nonsense, practical, functional approach? The Dasher dashes the old Volkswagen way of life.

"I believed in Volkswagen, and now Volkswagen doesn't believe in Volkswagen" is the lament of the faithful.

But VW is not to be detoured. "Different Volks for different folks" is the ad which best sums up the corporate attitude. Now VW has five separate car models flying the corporate flag.

Act Three is the dénouement. Is it possible that five models won't sell as well as one? It's not only possible, it happened.

From first place in imported cars, Volkswagen fell to fourth. Behind Toyota, Datsun and Honda. (To add insult to injury, Honda's theme "Keep it simple" seems to be lifted from Act One.)

In 1971 Volkswagen had 35 percent of the imported car market. By 1979 they were down to 12 percent.

The pattern of early success followed by line extension followed by disillusionment is fairly common. After all, you can't expect companies like Scott and Volkswagen to rest on their laurels. You'd expect them

An amusing headline for an automobile advertisement and a terrible strategy for an automobile company. The numbers alone are shocking. In 1965, Volkswagen was focused on one model, the Beetle, and had 67 percent of the imported car market. Then they line-extended and by 1993, their market share was less than 3 percent. Recently, of course, they brought back the Beetle and sales soared. Left unanswered is the question, what would have happened if Volkswagen focused on the Beetle and continued to improve the car as the years rolled by?

to find new fields to conquer. So how do they go about finding them? One way is obvious. They develop a new concept or a new product with a new position and a new name to match.

Volvo started to take off when they forgot luxury and driving and dependability and decided to focus on safety. Currently Volvo sells 400,000 cars worldwide and owns the safety position in the mind of the car buyer. (Unfortunately, Volvo is now driving the wrong way with convertibles and coupes.) BMW used exactly the same strategy in establishing the driving position. (The ultimate driving machine.)

What's a Volvo?

Many companies practice a more suitable form of line extension. They don't extend the line. They extend the concept behind the product.

Take Volvo, for example. What's a Volvo?

Like many auto brands, Volvo has had trouble recently. Volvo used to own the reliability position for larger imported cars. (A big dependable Beetle, if you will.)

Volvos got expensive and Volvo started selling luxury sedans and driving cars and safety cars and even a station wagon. Volvo became "the working car for the leisure class."

So what's a Volvo today? It's a dependable, luxurious, safety car that's fun to drive. But the more the merrier doesn't apply to positions. Four positions aren't better than one.

So Volvo sales go down as the curse of conceptual line extension claims another victim.

A Name Is a Rubber Band

It will stretch, but not beyond a certain point. Furthermore, the more you stretch a name, the weaker it becomes. (Just the opposite of what you might expect.)

How far should you stretch a name? This is an economics call as much as a judgment call.

Let's say you have a line of canned vegetables. Do you have a brand name for peas, another for corn and still a third for string beans? Probably not. Economically, it wouldn't make sense.

So Del Monte is probably right to use the same brand name on its line of canned fruits and vegetables. But notice what happens when a competitor zeroes in on a single product. The Dole line of canned pineapple.

Dole versus Del Monte in pineapple is no contest. Dole wins every time.

So what does Dole do next? It puts the Dole name on fresh bananas. The Dole banana.

Let's say Dole is successful in making Dole mean bananas. So what happens to pineapple? It's the teeter-totter principle with bananas on one side and pineapple on the other.

But can't Dole do what Del Monte did? Become a full-line supplier of canned and fresh food products?

Sure, but only at the expense of sacrificing its valuable pineapple franchise. And with the added disadvantage of being the last to line-extend.

Rules of the Road

We call line extension a "trap," not a mistake. Line extension can work if . . .

But it's a big if. If your competitors are foolish. If your volume is small. If you have no competitors. If you don't expect to build a position in the prospect's mind. If you don't do any advertising.

The truth is, many products are sold, few are positioned.

That is, the customer will pick up a can of peas without having a going-in preference, or position, for a brand of peas. In this case, any well-known brand name is going to do better than any unknown name.

And if you work for a company with thousands of small-volume products (3M is a typical example), you obviously cannot have a new name for every one.

So we offer some rules of the road that will tell you when to use the house name and when not to.

Here's what has happened many times to us. We'd be giving a speech about the dangers of line extension and nobody in the audience would be taking notes. Then we would announce that we were now going to tell them when a company could successfully line-extend. And everybody in the audience immediately picked up their pens and pencils. Line extension is what a company and its management want to do. We can understand that mindset because it's the basis of positioning thinking: It's hard to change a mind once a mind has been made up. And that's just as true for a mind that has decided that line extension is the way to go.

1. Expected volume. Potential winners should not bear the house name. Small-volume products should.

2. Competition. In a vacuum, the brand should not bear the house name. In a crowded field, it should.

3. Advertising support. Big-budget brands should not bear the house name. Small-budget brands should.

4. Significance. Breakthrough products should not bear the house name. Commodity products such as chemicals should.

5. Distribution. Off-the-shelf items should not bear the house name. Items sold by sales reps should.

14 Positioning a Company: Monsanto

You can position anything. A person, a product, a politician. Even a company.

Why would anyone want to position a company? Aside from a few acquisition-oriented corporations, who buys a company? And why would a company want to sell itself? To whom?

The Buying and Selling of Companies

Actually, a lot of buying and selling of companies is going on. Only it's called different names.

When a new employee accepts a job, he or she "buys" the company. (With its recruiting programs, a company is actually selling itself.)

Whom would you rather work for, General Electric or the Schenectady Electrical Works?

Every year companies across the country compete for top graduates at the nation's leading universities. Who do you think gets the cream of the crop?

That's right. The companies that occupy the best

positions in the minds of the prospective employee. The General Electrics, the Procter & Gambles.

And when someone buys a share of stock, what they are really paying for is a piece of that company's position, now and in the future.

How much a person is willing to pay for that stock (six or sixty times earnings) depends on the strength of that position in the buyer's mind.

Positioning a company effectively has lots of advantages if you happen to be an officer or director of that corporation. It's not easy, though.

The Name Problem Again

First of all, the name. Especially the name. Would you believe that Pullman doesn't happen to be much of a factor in the railroad car business anymore?

And that bus revenues represent only a small part of Greyhound's total sales?

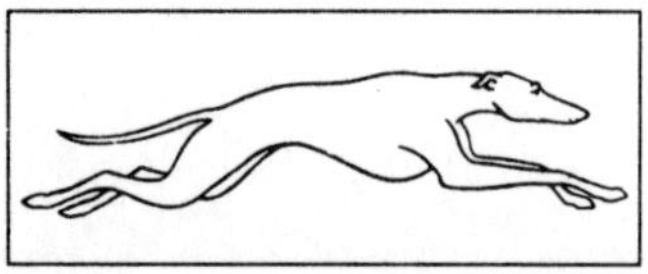

Greyhound spent millions trying to tell investors that it was "more than a bus company." And what is Greyhound today? It's a bus company. Period. It never pays to try to change a mind.

Both Pullman and Greyhound have changed drastically. Yet the way they are perceived by the public has scarcely changed at all. Their names have locked them to their past reputations.

Yet they have tried. Especially Greyhound, which has spent millions of dollars telling the financial coummunity that it is "more than a bus company."

But as long as those buses with the long slim dogs on the side go zipping up and down the interstate highways, the corporate advertising is an expensive mistake. If Greyhound wants to be more than a bus company, it needs a new name. A "more than a bus company" name.

But even with the right name, the corporate positioning job isn't done. Your company's name ought to stand for something within your industry.

Standing for Something

Consider Ford. Everyone knows that Ford is an automobile company. But what kind of car is a Ford?

Ford can't build a corporate position on a specific kind of car, because it builds them in all types and all sizes, including trucks. (Whether it should or not is another matter.)

So the positioning question boils down to some quality to be found across the board in all vehicles.

The company has settled on "innovation" as the key attribute in a vehicle from Ford. Result: the "Ford has a better idea" campaign.

Ford had a better idea and switched to its current "Quality is Job 1" campaign. Who owns the "quality" position in automobiles today? Our guess would be Mercedes-Benz. It never pays to try to take somebody else's position away from them.

Not bad, but many corporate programs settle on a mundane and hackneyed approach. Of which the most mundane and hackneyed, perhaps, is one based on people.

"Our people are our greatest resource."

"Gulf people: Meeting the challenge."

"Grumman: We're proud of the many products we make. We're prouder of the people who make them."

Are there no differences in quality between the people in one company and those in another?

Of course there are. But it's quite another matter to build a position based on better people.

Rightly or wrongly, the bigger, more successful companies have the better people. And the smaller, less successful companies have the leftovers.

GM

MARK OF EXCELLENCE

Nor have the corporate campaigns run by General Motors, most notably its Mark of Excellence advertising, done much for the company either. When your brands (Saturn, Chevrolet, Pontiac, Oldsmobile, Buick and Cadillac) don't incorporate the corporate name, a corporate advertising program is usually a waste.

So if your company occupies the top rung of the product ladder in the prospect's mind, you can be sure that the prospect will also think that your company has the best people.

If you're not on top and you tell the prospect you have the better people . . . Well, that's one of those inconsistencies that doesn't usually get resolved in your favor.

"If you're so smart, how come you're not rich?" It's a question that bears repeating.

If Ford really has the better ideas, why doesn't it use them in the marketplace to overtake General Motors instead of using them in its advertising to impress the public?

If Chrysler really has the better engineering, why doesn't it engineer better cars? And then use the better cars to outsell both Ford and General Motors?

These are not questions of fact. (Ford could have the better ideas and still be in second place.) These are questions that spring up in the prospect's mind.

And your advertising, to be successful, must answer these questions.

Besides, is it really so far-fetched to think that the bigger companies have the better people?

Our sympathies go to the underdogs, but our résumés get sent to the overdogs.

Diversification Is Not the Answer

Next to "people," the most common corporate positioning theme is "diversification." Companies want to become known as diversified manufacturers of a wide range of high-quality products.

Diversification is also ineffective as a corporate approach. As a matter of fact, the two concepts of positioning and diversification are poles apart.

It's a fact of life that strong positions in the prospect's mind are built on major achievements. Not on broad product lines.

General Electric is known as the world's largest electrical manufacturer. Not as a diversified maker of industrial, transportation, chemical and appliance products.

Even though General Electric makes thousands of consumer and industrial products, most of their successful products have been electrical ones. Most of their unsuccessful ones have been nonelectrical products. Computers being a typical example.

General Motors is known as the world's largest builder of automobiles. Not as a diversified maker of industrial, transportation and appliance products.

IBM has a reputation as the world's largest computer manufacturer. Not as a worldwide manufacturer of many types of office machines.

A company may be able to make more money by diversifying. It should think twice, however, about trying to build a position based on that concept.

Even the stock market consistently undervalues conglomerates like International Telephone & Telegraph and Gulf + Western. A typical example is Kaiser Industries, a holding company which controlled a number of operating companies. The market price of

We were talking about "diversification" as an advertising theme. but the truth is that diversification turned out to make no business sense either. ITT was a typical example of a company that floundered until it was broken up into three separate companies. This concept is explored is more detail in a book called *Focus: The Future of Your Company Depends on It.*

Kaiser Industries was consistently lower than the net value of its parts. After Kaiser was split up, stockholders received $21 for shares that sold at $12.

Sometimes companies think they are concentrating their communication efforts when they are really not. The positioning concept becomes so broad that it is almost meaningless.

Which company calls itself "a developer and supplier of information systems for work, education and entertainment?"

Would you believe Bell & Howell? That's right, Bell & Howell.

The Monsanto Approach

A good place to start a corporate positioning program is with a clear, concise definition of what a company is. But the best corporate positioning programs go beyond just a definition. The best programs do the job with actions, not just words. Or sometimes the words themselves represent the action.

As an example, let's discuss a corporate positioning program run recently by Monsanto.

Objective: To make Monsanto the leader and spokesperson for the industry. (Undefined, for the moment is what industry we are talking about.)

So, how do you get to be a leader?

We believe that history shows that companies get to be a leader by being the first to do something. Not just by claiming leadership.

IBM was first to market computers, Xerox was first to market plain-paper copiers, DuPont was first to market nylon. What could Monsanto be the first to do?

A company like Monsanto had three possible areas where it could establish a leadership position. Let's look at each possibility in turn.

1. Product leadership. Where does Monsanto rank in product leadership?

Rather well, according to a recent research study among college graduates with annual incomes of $15,000 and over. Monsanto is not a General Motors. Nor is it an American Motors. Rather, Monsanto is somewhere in between.

DuPont	81 percent
Dow	66 percent
Monsanto	63 percent
Union Carbide	57 percent
Allied Chemical	34 percent
American Cyanamid	29 percent
Olin	25 percent
FMC	13 percent

(Note how the initial company, FMC, is at the bottom of the list. Not untypical.)

Actually, Monsanto, Dow and Union Carbide are clustered together in second place, with the differences statistically not very significant.

Second to whom? Why DuPont, of course.

DuPont is another IBM, Xerox or Chivas Regal.

With product achievements like Teflon, nylon and Dacron, DuPont is tough.

A company has no hope of establishing product leadership by going head-to-head against DuPont.

Futhermore, many of the companies are running corporate programs emphasizing product leadership. Union Carbide, Olin, FMC and others.

2. Business Leadership. Now, let's look at the second possible approach, business leadership, which today essentially means defending the free-enterprise system.

Could Monsanto be the first to speak up for free enterprise?

Obviously not. The Advertising Council, in cooperation with the U.S. Department of Commerce and the U.S. Department of Labor, launched a massive program in 1976 to explain the "American economic system and your part in it."

You know it was a massive program because they lined up Charles Schulz to do the "Peanuts" cartoons to illustrate the material.

Starting with the Warner & Swasey campaign, which is now more than 40 years old, many companies have also been speaking up for the system.

Textron has run a television campaign to explain "how private enterprise works at Textron."

"In these days, when declining faith in many of our institutions is reported, business has an obligation to explain how it contributes to our society," said G. William Miller, Textron's chairman before he became Secretary of the Treasury.

Allied Chemical has also run a print campaign with the theme, "Profits are for people."

"The babel of economic advertising," said *The New York Times* in commenting negatively on the flurry of free enterprise programs.

It's a basic principle of positioning to avoid the areas that everyone else is talking about. The fad, if you will. To make progress, a company has to strike out on its own into new, unexplored territory.

3. Industry Leadership. Which left the third approach, industry leadership. Could Monsanto improve its leadership position in the chemical industry?

One thing was perfectly obvious when Monsanto first considered a corporate program. Chemicals were under attack. The public was being fed a daily diet of bad chemical news. In newspapers and magazines. On radio and television.

The message was coming through loud and clear: "Chemicals cause cancer."

An irrational, antichemical mood was sweeping the country. This comment on NBC Nightly News (September 4, 1976) was typical: "On one point there's almost total agreement. The chance now of serious chemical accidents is far greater than the chance of nuclear accidents."

And the problem was serious. According to Yankelovich, Skelly and White, a highly regarded opinion research firm: "The chemical industry stands out as a principal villain in terms of being a major souce of health problems."

Chemical Facts of Life

What Monsanto decided to do was to speak up about chemicals. To tell the public about the benefits of chemicals as well as the risks.

"Without chemicals, life itself would be impossi-

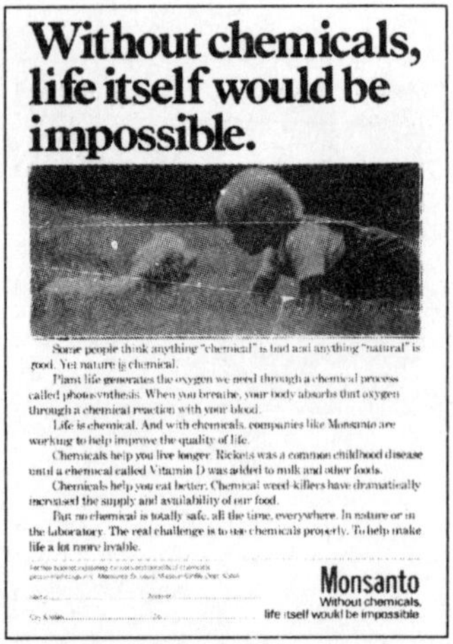

This was the first advertisement in the Monsanto "Chemical Facts of Life" program.

ble" was the theme of the Monsanto program. The first ad stated the message as follows:

> Some people think anything "chemical" is bad and anything "natural" is good. Yet nature *is* chemical.
>
> Plant life generates the oxygen we need through a chemical process called photosynthesis. When you breathe, your body absorbs that oxygen through a chemical reaction with your blood.
>
> Life is chemical. And with chemicals, companies like Monsanto are working to help improve the quality of life.
>
> Chemicals help you live longer. Rickets was a common childhood disease until a chemical called Vitamin D was added to milk and other foods.
>
> But no chemical is totally safe, all the time, everywhere. In nature or in the laboratory. The real challenge is to use chemicals properly. To help make life a lot more livable.

Why Monsanto? Why should Monsanto speak up for what is essentially an industry problem?

The answer goes back to the positioning strategy. To be recognized as the leader of the chemical industry, Monsanto had to do what the leader should do.

That is, speak for the industry. By waiting for others to do so first, Monsanto would forfeit its opportunity to assume the leadership mantle.

Monsanto Gets the Credit

In life, timing is everything. An analysis of the chemical situation back in 1976 indicated that the pendulum was ready to swing back. Public opinion was likely to be more favorably inclined toward chemical companies in the future than it was at the time. Whether Monsanto did anything or not.

Naturally, a "chemical facts of life" program could accelerate the swing. And Monsanto would be given a good share of the credit.

Which is exactly what happened. The pendulum did swing. The positive attitudes among the general public, according to one survey, increased from 36 percent to 42 percent in less than two years, a substantial increase. (In the same period positive attitudes toward the oil industry declined from 37 percent to 22 percent. Which indicates what can happen when rising prices combine with the lack of an adequate explanation on the part of an industry.)

Even *The New York Times* has started to come around. In an editorial about saccharin entitled, "The Case of the Useful Carcinogen," the newspaper commented, "The trouble with an absolute ban is that it leaves no room for balancing benefits against risks."

The ultimate accolade for Monsanto's role came in a 1979 *Business Week* article entitled, "Cleansing the Chemical Image."

"The chemical industry's movement into the image-building arena," said the magazine, "was spearheaded by Monsanto Co. in 1977. Chairman John W. Hanley saw that chemicals came out the villain every time and decided it was time to do something. That year, the company spent $4.5 million on image building, and it has equaled or exceeded that amount each year since.

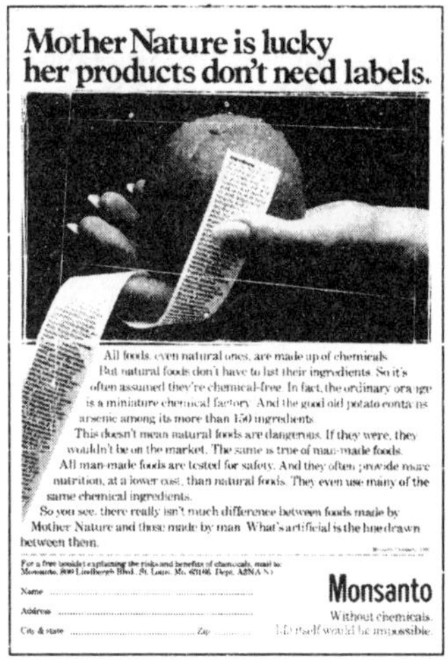

The second advertisement in the series listed the hundreds of chemicals in an ordinary orange.

Monsanto shifted its focus from chemicals to genetically engineered products. Turns out that they should have stayed in chemicals.

Business Week also noted the company's leadership role. "Following Monsanto's lead," said the magazine, "DuPont Co. committed $4 million to an instititutional advertising campaign of its own."

In the business of corporate positioning, the perception of leadership is something you can cash at the bank. Whether you're a chemical company, a bank or an automobile manufacturer, when your customers are impressed, you will always do better than your competitors.

15 Positioning a Country: Belgium

With the advent of relatively inexpensive airfare, we're fast becoming a world of tourists.

In days gone by, international travel was limited to the older, more affluent person. Today that's all changed. There was a time when the flight attendants were young and the travelers old. Now the travelers are young and the flight attendants are old.

The Sabena Situation

One of the 16 major North Atlantic carriers jockeying for these international travelers is an airline called Sabena Belgian World Airlines. But all competitors don't compete on an equal basis. TWA and Pan Am, for example, have for some time had a long list of gateway cities in both the United States and Europe.

But a few years back, Sabena had only one place to generate traffic from. New York. So if you weren't going to make a connection in Brussels, you were on the wrong airline. Unless there was a hijacker aboard, every Sabena plane was going to land in Belgium.

While Sabena captured the lion's share of the traffic to Belgium, they were on a very meager diet. Not too many people were flying to this little country.

These statistics are virtually unchanged in 20 years. The top five Eurpean destinations are still the United Kingdom, Germany, France, The Netherlands, and Italy. The only change is that The Netherlands has moved to fourth place and Italy dropped to fifth place.

In a recent year, here were the percentages of North Atlantic passengers flying to the 16 leading countries:

United Kingdom	29 percent
Germany	15 percent
France	10 percent
Italy	9 percent
Netherlands	6 percent
Spain	5 percent
Ireland	5 percent
Portugal	4 percent
Switzerland	3 percent
Iceland	3 percent
Israel	3 percent
Denmark	3 percent
Greece	2 percent
Belgium	2 percent
Norway	1 percent
Sweden	1 percent

On the country ladder in the prospective traveler's mind, Belgium was on one of the bottom rungs. If it was on the ladder at all.

One look at these numbers and it was easy to tell what was wrong with Sabena's advertising. Sabena was using classic airline strategy. Sell the food and the service.

"Do I have to be a bon vivant to fly Sabena?" said a typical ad. But all the terrific food in the world won't induce you to fly an airline that isn't going where you want to go.

Napoleon met his Waterloo in Belgium, but few people know that. When we were taken on a guided tour of the country, the Sabena advertising manager refused to take us to Waterloo. "Nobody cares about war," he said. Nobody in Belgium maybe, but not in the United States. Six million people a year visit Gettysburg, one of America's favorite tourist destinations.

Position the Country, Not the Airline

Sabena's most productive strategy was obviously not to position the airline but to position the country. In other words, do what KLM had done for Amsterdam.

Sabena had to make Belgium a place where a traveler would want to spend some time. Not a place you traveled through to get to somewhere else.

Furthermore, there's a moral here that shines through loud and clear. Whether you're selling colas, companies or countries. Out of mind, out of business.

Most Americans knew very little about Belgium. They thought Waterloo was a suburb of Paris and the most important product of Belgium was waffles. Many didn't even know where the country was.

"If it's Tuesday, this must be Belgium," said it all.

But how do you find a position for a country? Well, if you think about it, the most successful countries all have strong mental images.

Say "England" and people think of pageantry, Big Ben and the Tower of London.

Say "Italy" and they think of the Coliseum and St. Peter's and works of art.

Say "Amsterdam" and it's tulips, Rembrandt and those wonderful canals.

Say "France" and it's food and the Eiffel Tower and the dazzling Riviera.

Your mind sees places as mental picture postcards. Take cities, for example. In your mind, New York is probably a skyline of tall buildings. San Francisco is cable cars and the Golden Gate Bridge. Cleveland is a gray place with a lot of industrial smokestacks.

Obviously, London, Paris and Rome are all top-of-the-ladder destinations that are the most popular with first-time travelers to Europe. Sabena had little chance to get these travelers.

But in the United States there is a large segment of seasoned travelers looking to visit the next tier of destinations. Countries like Greece with its ruins. Switzerland with its mountains.

Once the objective became clear, finding a position wasn't that difficult.

Beautiful Belgium

The Castle of the Counts, one of Belgium's many visually interesting tourist sites.

Belgium is a very beautiful country with many of the things that appeal to the seasoned European traveler. Like interesting cities, historical palaces, museums and art galleries.

Oddly enough, the Belgians didn't really have a very high opinion of their own country as a tourist attraction. That attitude is perhaps epitomized by a sign that used to be at the Brussels airport. Among other things it said, "Welcome to Belga country. Weather: mild, but rains 220 days a year, on average."

As the result, their favorite tourist strategy was to promote the central location of Belgium and the ease of getting somewhere else. Like London, Paris and Rome. (If you want to visit New York, fly to Philadelphia because it's close by.)

Little thought was really being given to making Belgium a tourist attraction. A brief stroll around downtown Brussels told it all. As you walked into the Grand Place, with its goldleaf facade, probably the most beautiful square in all of Europe, you would discover that the entire center of it was being used as a parking lot. (Cars were eventually banned from the square.)

The Grand Place, still the most beautiful square in all of Europe.

There's an important lesson here. The perceptions of people living in a place are often different from those visiting it.

Many New Yorkers fail to see New York as a tourist attraction. They remember the garbage strikes and forget the Statue of Liberty. Yet New York attracts 16 million visitors a year who all want to see those "big buildings."

Three-Star Cities

But while "beautiful" was nice, it wasn't really enough as a tourist promotion theme. To position a country as a destination, you need attractions that will keep the traveler around for at least a few days.

Nobody considers Monaco a destination because its number one attraction, Monte Carlo, can be seen in an evening. (Monaco's number two attraction, Princess Grace, can't be seen at all.)

Obviously, size is an important factor. Big countries have lots of attractions. Small countries are at a disadvantage. (If the Grand Canyon ran through Belgium, you wouldn't have much land left to look at.)

Nothing much has changed in 20 years. Tournai lost a star and the Benelux edition of the Michelin Guide has been split in two. There's now one for Belgium and Luxembourg and one for The Netherlands. There's still only one three-star city in The Netherlands. So Belgium now leads Holland four to one. A marketing program is much more effective if it is based on "credentials" provided by an objective third party.

The answer to the size problem was found in one of those famous Michelin Guides. You may not know that Michelin rates cities as well as restaurants.

The Benelux edition lists six three-star "worth a special journey" cities. Five were in Belgium: Bruges, Ghent, Antwerp, Brussels and Tournai.

But what was really surprising was the fact that the big tourist attraction to the North, Holland, had only one three-star city, Amsterdam.

The ad that resulted was headlined, "In beautiful Belgium, there are five Amsterdams." The illustration was comprised of five beautiful four-color pictures of Belgium's three-star cities.

This advertisement generated an enormous number of inquiries about a country many travelers had seen only through a train window as they traveled from Amsterdam to Paris.

One of the inquiries came in the form of a call from the minister of tourism in Holland to his counterpart in Belgium.

Needless to say, there was one irate Dutchman who wanted that advertisement killed, along with the people who created it.

The "three-star city" strategy had three important things going for it.

First, it related Belgium to a destination that was already in the mind of the traveler, Amsterdam. In any positioning program, if you can start with a strongly held perception, you'll be that much ahead in your efforts to establish your own position. Second, the Michelin Guide, another entity already in the mind of the traveler, gave the concept credibility.

Finally, the "five cities to visit" made Belgium a bona fide destination.

Eventually the "three-star cities of beautiful Belgium" concept was moved into television. The response was substantial.

A television commercial with its ability to communicate in sight and sound can drive pictures of a country into the mind much more quickly than a print advertisement.

There's also a danger of misusing the medium of television. This happens when your visuals are similar to other visuals being used by competing countries.

Think about those islands in the Caribbean you've seen advertised. Can you keep those palm trees and beaches separate in your mind? Do you conjure up the same mental postcard when someone says Nassau, the Virgin Islands or Barbados? If there's no difference, the mind will simply dump all those visuals in a slot marked "Islands in the Caribbean" and tune out.

The same can happen with those quaint European villages. Or the smiling residents waving mugs of beer at you. One windmill is worth a thousand street scenes, no matter how cleverly directed.

Pictures alone won't build a position in the mind. Only words will do that. To create an effective positioning program, you have to "verbalize the visuals." Alliteration can also be an effective memory device in this process.

What Happened?

Now you might be wondering why, after all this, you haven't seen much about Belgium and its three-star cities.

A number of events kept this program from ever being fully implemented. All of which holds a lesson for anyone embarked on a positioning program.

Today, not too many people fly on Sabena or visit Belgium unless they happen to work for the European Community. It's too bad. "Beautiful Belgium" could have been a powerful tourist positioning program, but it would have needed several decades of consistent publicity and advertising to accomplish that objective. If we have learned one thing in 20 years, it's the power of consistency.

First, an organizational change took place at Sabena just as the television program was being developed. New management was not committed to the program, and when headquarters in Brussels wanted to revive the "gateway to Europe" strategy, they quickly acquiesced.

The lesson here is that a successful positioning program requires a major long-term commitment by the people in charge. Whether it's the head of a corporation, a church or an airline. Winning the mind of a traveler is a lot like waging a war. Everyone in the army, from the top down, must agree on what the objective is.

Another problem was the Belgian Tourist Office which, for political reasons, could never understand why other cities couldn't be part of the program, even though they didn't rate three stars.

In this overcommunicated society, the only hope is the simple idea. Bringing in other cities would only confuse and complicate the issue.

The lesson here is that positioning may require you to oversimplify your communications. So be it. There is no other way. Confusion is the enemy. Simplicity is the holy grail.

16 Positioning a Product: Milk Duds

The brand is Milk Duds, a product of Beatrice Foods. Milk Duds is a candy product that comes in a little yellow and brown box. It had a reputation as a "movie" candy, but Beatrice Foods wanted to broaden its Milk Duds business down to the younger, candy-oriented crowd.

Milk Duds, a chocolate-coated caramel candy that comes in a box.

The First Step

The first step in any positioning program is to look inside the mind of the prospect.

And who is the prospect for Milk Duds? It's not some little kid who doesn't know the score. Research indicates that the best Milk Duds prospect is a sophisticated candy buyer. He or she has been in and out of candy stores several hundred times at least.

The average Milk Duds prospect is 10 years old. A cautious, suspicious, shrewd purchasing agent who is always on the lookout for value received.

Most positioning programs are nothing more or

The 10-year-old kid became the target for Milk Duds advertising. Isolating a narrow target is usually the first step in finding an effective position. While a product like Milk Duds might appeal to everybody (and it does), it's usually a mistake to try to appeal to everybody in your advertising. Let adults get the message indirectly.

less than a search for the obvious. Yet the obvious is easy to miss if you zero in too quickly on the product itself. (As with the "purloined letter" of Edgar Allan Poe, the obvious is often hard to find because it's too easy to see. It's too obvious.)

What's in the prospect's mind when the subject of candy comes up? Not Milk Duds, even though the average 10-year-old kid might be vaguely aware of the brand.

For most 10-year-olds, the candy urge immediately conjures up the concept of candy bars.

Candy bars like Hersheys, Nestlés, Mounds, Almond Joys, Reeses, Snickers, Milky Ways. Put there, of course, by the millions of dollars' worth of advertising spent on these and other candy bar brands.

Repositioning the Competition

Since Milk Duds was getting only a small fraction of that kind of advertising money, it would have been hopeless to try to build an identity for the brand. The only way to drive Milk Duds into the kid's mind was to find a way to reposition the candy-bar category.

In other words, find a way to make the millions of dollars spent by the competition work for Milk Duds by setting up the brand as a better alternative to the candy bar. (Little would be gained by just putting another candy name in an overloaded mind.)

Fortunately, there was a glaring weakness in the candy-bar competition that could be exploited. And the weakness is obvious once you look at the size and shape and price of today's Hershey bar.

A candy bar just doesn't last very long. A kid can go through a 30-cent Hershey bar in 2.3 seconds flat.

There exists a strong undercurrent of dissatisfaction among America's candy eaters. As the candy bar has shrunk in size, this discontent has grown.

"My hard-earned allowance doesn't last very long when it comes to candy bars."

"Either I'm eating faster or candy bars are getting smaller."

"You can suck up a candy bar awfully fast these days!"

This is the soft, chocolaty underbelly of the candy-bar competition.

Milk Duds are different. They come in a box instead of a package. They give the kid 15 individual slow-eating chocolate-covered caramels.

Compared with a candy bar, a box of Milk Duds will last a long time. (If you try to stuff a whole box in your mouth, it will cement your jaws shut.) Which is exactly why the product has been so popular in movie theaters.

So what is Milk Duds' new position?

The Long-Lasting Alternative

Why, it's America's long-lasting alternative to the candy bar.

If this seems like the obvious answer to you, it wasn't to the people who used to do the Milk Duds advertising. In some 15 years of Milk Duds' television commercials, there wasn't one reference to the long-lasting idea.

Some scenes from the television commercial that launched the Milk Duds "long lasting" position. Unfortunately the chairman didn't like the Big Mouth and killed the program. Milk Duds went back to the movies.

Let's take a mental walk through a 30-second TV commercial to see how the long-lasting idea was sugarcoated for the benefit of the 10-year-old.

1. Once there was a kid who had a big mouth . . . (A kid is standing next to an enormous mouth.)

2. . . . that loved candy bars. (The kid is shoveling candy bars one right after another into the mouth.)

3. . . . but they didn't last very long. (The kid runs out of candy bars and the mouth gets very upset.)

4. Then he discovered chocolaty caramel Milk Duds. (The kid holds up the Milk Duds, and the mouth starts to lick its chops.)

5. The mouth loved the Milk Duds because they last a long time. (The kid rolls the Milk Duds one by one up the mouth's tongue.)

6. (Then the kid and the mouth sing a duet together, which is the campaign song.) When a candy bar is only a memory, you'll still be eating your Milk Duds.

7. Get your mouth some Milk Duds. (Big smiles on both the kid and the mouth.)

Did it work?

Not only did the television advertising reverse a downward sales trend, but in the ensuing months Beatrice Foods sold more Milk Duds than it ever did in its history.

If there is one lesson to be learned from the Milk Duds example, it's this: The solution to a positioning problem is usually found in the prospect's mind, not in the product.

17 Positioning a Service: Mailgram

What's the difference between the positioning of a product (like Milk Duds) and the positioning of a service (like Western Union's Mailgram)?

Not much, especially from a strategic point of view. Most of the differences are in techniques.

The Mailgram was a joint service of Western Union and the U.S. Postal Service.

Visual vs. Verbal

In a product ad, the dominant element is usually the picture, the visual element. In a service ad, the dominant element is usually the words, the verbal element. (So if you saw an advertisement with a big picture of an automobile, you would assume the car was being advertised, not a car rental service.)

With a product like Milk Duds, the primary medium was television, a visually oriented vehicle.

With a service like Mailgram, the primary medium was radio, a verbally oriented vehicle.

Naturally, there are a lot of exceptions to these principles. If everyone knows what the product looks

Visuals can be extremely memorable, but unless they are connected to a verbal idea they lose their effectiveness. Who can ever forget O.J. Simpson running through airport terminals, but what was the message that Hertz was trying to communicate? Who knows?

like, there is no advantage in using print, television or other forms of visual media.

Conversely, if a service can make effective use of a visual symbol (O. J. Simpson for Hertz, for example), then visual media can often be productive.

In spite of the exceptions, it's surprising how often these visual/verbal generalities hold up. In a four-way test of newspapers, magazines, radio and television for Mailgram, the most effective medium was radio. But the essence of the Mailgram story is strategy, not media. Before discussing strategy, it may be helpful to take a look at how the system works.

Electronic Mail

Developed jointly with the U.S. Postal Service and inaugurated on a limited experimental basis in 1970, Mailgram is the nation's first electronic mail.

To send a Mailgram, you call Western Union, which transmits the message electronically to a post office near the recipient. The Mailgram is delivered the next business day.

To show how technologically advanced the system is, let's follow a typical Mailgram being sent from New York to the West Coast.

1. The New York customer reaches for the telephone and calls Western Union.

2. An operator in one of Western Union's central telephone answering bureaus, open around the clock, takes the customer's message and feeds it into a computerized video display unit.

3. After verifying the message and destination with the customer, the operator pushes a button which automatically sends the message to a master computer in Middletown, Virginia.

4. The computer processes the message and relays it to an earth station in Glenwood, New Jersey.

5. From there the message goes up in space 22,300 miles to a Westar satellite in synchronous orbit about the equator.

6. From Westar, the message is then relayed to an earth station in Steele Valley, California.

7. From the earth station, the message goes by land line (or microwave) to the post office nearest the addressee, where it is printed out on a high-speed Teletype machine.

8. The message is then inserted in a special blue and white envelope and delivered by regular letter carrier to the California recipient.

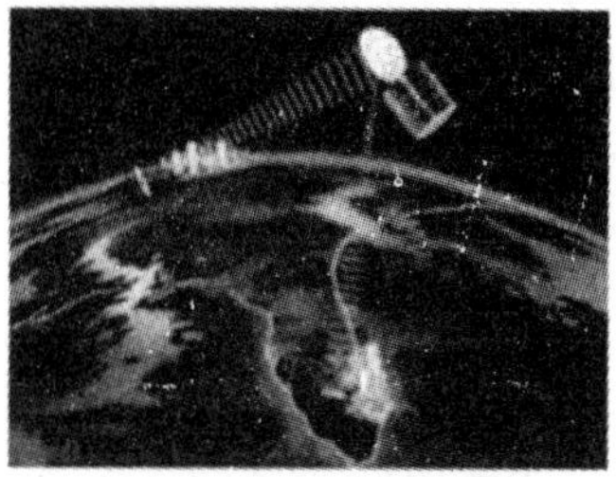

This is the Westar satellite that played a key role in the Mailgram system. Later we tried strenuously to get Western Union to change its name to Westar Corporation. They refused and later the company went bankrupt. Would a name change have helped? We think so. (Today, of course, the Western Union brand survives as a money transfer service, a shadow of its former glory.)

In addition to sending Mailgrams by telephone, the customer can also send them by Telex, TWX, magnetic tape, computer, facsimile equipment or communicating typewriters.

Why belabor the technicalities? Why discuss the complex details of the Mailgram system?

To make an important point. Most advertising programs never go beyond the details of the product or service which is offered for sale. And the more interesting and complex the service is, the more likely this will happen. The marketing people who are responsible for introducing the product get all wrapped up in the service and forget all about the customer. As a matter of fact, the traditional approach would have been to introduce Mailgram as a "new, automated, computerized electronic communication service" or something of that sort. (Western Union spent millions on computer programming alone, not to mention the enormous expense of earth stations, satellites, etc.)

The Low-Cost Telegram

You can't walk away from what's already in the prospect's mind. When you said "Western Union," most people thought "telegram."

Regardless of how much money you spend, regardless of how technologically interesting your service is, to get inside the prospect's mind, you have to relate to what's already there. You can't walk away from it.

And what's up there in the prospect's mind? The Telegram, of course.

Anytime you mention the word "Western Union," the average mind conjures up the most famous yellow message in the history of the world. And the "gram" part of the Mailgram name only reinforces this perception.

So what's the difference between the new gram and the old gram?

Well, the main difference is price. Both have the same telegraphic format. Both demand immediate attention. But the yellow Telegram message is three times the price of the new blue and white Mailgram message.

So the original positioning theme developed for Mailgram was simple: "Mailgram: Impact of a Telegram at a fraction of the cost."

At this point, someone said "Wait a minute. Why

position Mailgram against the Telegram, also a Western Union service? Why take business away from ourselves?

"Furthermore, the Telegram is a declining business. Why compare a new, modern service like Mailgram with an old service past its prime? The Telegram still has an important role to play, but it is not a growth business."

Publicly we said that the "Telegram still has an important role to play," but privately we told the Western Union chairman that the service was a dead duck. Advertising agencies have to be more diplomatic than that which is one reason that we are now marketing consultants.

The logic is impeccable. But as often happens, logic is not necessarily the best strategy for dealing with human minds. Still, the logic was so sound, it was worthwhile rethinking the concept. Especially since there was another positioning strategy that also had merit.

The High-Speed Letter

Actually the name itself suggests a second positioning approach. We could relate the Mailgram to the U.S. mail.

Then, too, if Western Union wanted the Mailgram to take business away from another service, the numbers suggest it would be much better to position the new service against regular mail.

In a recent year, 58 billion first-class letters were dropped into the nation's 69 million letter boxes. That's 840 first-class letters per household per year.

The Telegram generates only a tiny fraction of that kind of volume.

So a second theme was developed: "Mailgram: A new high-speed service for important messages."

Which is the better approach? In spite of the negatives, positioning theory suggests that the "low-cost Telegram" is a better direction than the "high-speed letter." Yet Mailgram was potentially too important to Western Union's future to make a decision based on judgment alone. So both campaigns were test-marketed using computer data to track results.

Low Cost vs. High Speed

The test itself was a massive one. No tiny markets like Peoria were even considered. The six Mailgram test cities were Boston, Chicago, Houston, Los Angeles, Philadelphia and San Francisco. All big, important communication centers.

Who won? Actually both campaigns were effective. Here are the data for Mailgram volume increases in the test cities during the 13-week program.

High-speed letter cities	plus 73%
Low-cost Telegram cities	plus 100%

These numbers alone were enough to prove the superiority of the "low-cost Telegram" position. But what really decided the issue were the product awareness levels in the test cities, which were measured both before the program ran and afterwards.

Here are the figures on how many people could correctly describe what a Mailgram was before the print and broadcast advertising began.

High-speed letter cities	27%
Low-cost Telegram cities	23%

Statistically, not much difference. This indicates that the cities were pretty evenly matched. In other words, about one-fourth of the market already knew.

After the advertising ran, however, there was a big difference in the two groups of cities. Here are the Mailgram awareness levels 13 weeks later.

High-speed letter cities	25%
Low-cost Telegram cities	47%

As unbelievable as it may seem, awareness in the high-speed letter cities actually declined. From 27 percent to 25 percent. (Not really statistically significant.)

Then where did the increased volume come from in the high-speed letter cities? Obviously from people who knew what a Mailgram was and were reminded to use the service by the advertising.

It was a totally different story in the low-cost Telegram cities. Mailgram awareness more than doubled. From 23 percent to 47 percent.

Not only was this a big jump, but the numbers also suggested that Mailgram volume increases in the low-cost Telegram cities were likely to continue over a much longer period of time.

A note about the Telegram itself. While the Mailgram was being test-marketed, Western Union also measured Telegram volume in the test cities before, during and after the advertising. They found that volume held fairly stable. Today the company feels that advertising the Mailgram as the low-cost Telegram has helped rather than hurt Telegram volume.

And what happened to Mailgram since the adver-

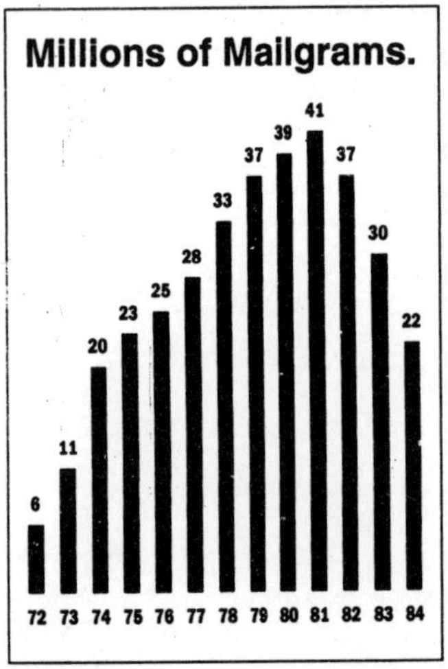

Western Union fired us in 1981 and hired another advertising agency which promptly dropped the "Impact of a Telegram" strategy. Mailgram volume fell substantially in each of the next three years. No product or service will live forever, of course. In the long run, the advance of fax and e-mail have made the Mailgram obsolete.

tising strategy was resolved? An overwhelming success. Mailgram is one of Western Union's most profitable services.

Revenues have increased substantially every year. In eight years Mailgram revenues went from $3 million to $80 million a year.

But one thing didn't change. That was the positioning concept behind the service. Every Mailgram print ad, television and radio commercial was built around the key concept: "Impact of a Telegram at a fraction of the cost."

18 Positioning a Long Island Bank

Like Western Union, banks sell a service and not a product. Unlike a Mailgram, however, which is a national service, banking is a regional service. By law, banks are generally restricted to a single state, county or even city.

In fact, positioning a bank is much like positioning a department store, an appliance store or any other kind of retail establishment. To successfully position a retail outlet, you must know the territory.

This is no longer true. Today Citibank, Chase, Bank of America, Wells Fargo, Bank One, and others are fighting to become national banks. History teaches us that only two of these banks will ultimately dominate the category. (The law of duality.)

The Long Island Banking Situation

To understand how a position for the Long Island Trust Company was developed, you should know a little bit about the territory.

For many years Long Island Trust was the leading bank on the Island. It was the largest bank, it had the most branches and it made the most money.

In the seventies, however, the bank battlefield on Long Island changed dramatically. A new law permitted unrestricted branch banking throughout New York State.

Since then, many of the big New York City banks have become firmly entrenched in the Long Island area. Banks like Citibank, Chase Manhattan and Chemical Bank.

Also, a good number of Long Island's residents commute to New York City everyday and do part of their banking at these same banks.

However, the intrusion of the big city banks into Long Island Trust's territory was only part of the problem. The territory that really counts is in the mind of the banking prospect. And a little research turned up a lot of bad news.

Mapping the Prospect's Mind

By now you can appreciate the importance of knowing what's in the prospect's mind. Not only about your product or service, but about competitive offerings as well.

Often the insights are intuitive. Nobody needs a $10,000 research project to know that Western Union is strongly identified with the Telegram. Nor was much research needed to determine the positions of Milk Duds, Belgium and Monsanto.

More often than not, however, it can be exceedingly helpful to map the prospect's mind by means of formal positioning research. Helpful not only in developing a strategy, but in selling the strategy to top management. (The chief executive who has spent 30 years with one company will obviously see that company differently than a prospect whose total exposure over the same 30 years can be measured in minutes or even seconds.)

"Mapping the prospect's mind" is normally done with a research technique called "semantic differential." This was the procedure used to develop a positioning program for the Long Island Trust Company.

In semantic differential research, the prospect is given a set of attributes and then asked to rank each competitor on a scale, generally from 1 to 10. For example, price might be one of the attributes. In automobiles, it's obvious that Cadillac would be ranked at the high end and Chevette at the low end.

In banking, there is almost no price perception, so other attributes were selected. The ones chosen were these: (1) many branches, (2) full range of services, (3) quality of service, (4) large capital, (5) helps Long Island residents and (6) helps Long Island economy. The first four attributes are the traditional reasons for doing business with a particular bank. The last two are unique to the Long Island situation.

As far as the traditional reasons were concerned, the situation was bleak for the Long Island Trust. Prospects rated them last on all four attributes.

Most marketing research is overly concerned with the attitudes of customers and prospects to the company itself. It doesn't really matter what customers think about your company and your products or services. The thing that counts is how your company compares with your competitors. That's why we have used semantic differential research extensively over the years.

Many branches

Chemical	7.3
National Bank of North America	6.7
European American	6.6
Chase Manhattan	6.4
Citibank	6.1
Long Island Trust	5.4

Full range of services	
Chemical	7.7
Citibank	7.7
Chase Manhattan	7.6
National Bank of North America	7.4
European American	7.3
Long Island Trust	7.0

Quality of service	
Chemical	7.2
Citibank	7.0
National Bank of North America	7.0
Chase Manhattan	6.9
European American	6.8
Long Island Trust	6.7

Large capital	
Chemical	8.2
Chase Manhattan	8.2
Citibank	8.1
National Bank of North America	7.8
European American	7.7
Long Island Trust	7.1

The positions were reversed, however, when the attributes concerned Long Island itself.

Helps Long Island residents	
Long Island Trust	7.5
National Bank of North America	6.6
European American	5.2
Chemical	5.1
Chase Manhattan	4.7
Citibank	4.5

Helps Long Island economy

Long Island Trust	7.3
National Bank of North America	6.7
European American	5.4
Chemical	5.4
Citibank	5.3
Chase Manhattan	4.9

When the attributes concerned Long Island, the Long Island Trust Company went right to the top. A not too surprising result, considering the power of the name.

Developing the Strategy

What approach should Long Island Trust take? Conventional wisdom says you accept your strengths and work on improving your weaknesses. In other words, run ads telling the prospects about the great service, friendly tellers, etc.

But conventional wisdom is not positioning thinking. Positioning theory says you must start with what the prospect is already willing to give you.

And the only thing the prospect gave Long Island Trust was the "Long Island position." Accepting this position allowed the bank to repel the invasion of the big city banks. The first ad stated the theme.

> Why send your money to the city if you live on the Island?
>
> It makes sense to keep your money close to home. Not at a city bank. But at Long Island Trust. Where it can work for Long Island.

The first advertisement in the Long Island Trust program. If we have learned anything in 20 years, it is that marketing programs like this one need a much heavier emphasis on publicity. We should have encouraged the chairman to do radio and television as well as print interviews. David versus Goliath is a sure-fire human-interest story.

> After all, we concentrate on developing Long Island.
>
> Not Manhattan Island. Or some island off Kuwait.
>
> Ask yourself, who do you think is most concerned about Long Island's future?
>
> A bank-come-lately with hundreds of other branches in the greater metropolitan area plus affiliates in five continents?
>
> Or a bank like ours that's been here for over 50 years and has 33 offices on Long Island.

A second ad had a photo of palm trees in front of a building with a Citibank N.A. sign.

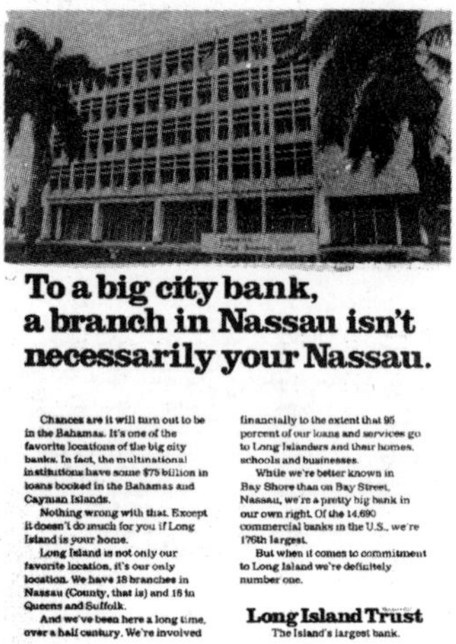

The second advertisement in the Long Island Trust series. To a home owner in Great Neck, Nassau is the county that collects the real estate taxes. To a banker in Manhattan, Nassau is an Island in the Bahamas.

> To a big city bank, a branch in Nassau isn't necessarily your Nassau.
>
> Chances are it will turn out to be in the Bahamas. It's one of the favorite locations of the big city banks. In fact, the multinational institutions have some $75 billion in loans booked in the Bahamas and Cayman Islands.
>
> Nothing wrong with that. Except it doesn't do much for you if Long Island is your home.
>
> Long Island is not only our favorite location, it's our only location. We have 18 branches in Nassau (County, that is) and 16 in Queens and Suffolk.
>
> And we've been here a long time, over a half century. We're involved financially to the extent that 95 percent of our loans and services go to Long Islanders and their homes, schools and businesses.

Other ads in the campaign had similar themes:

"The city is a great place to visit, but would you want to bank there?"

"To a city bank, the only island that really counts is Manhattan." (A tiny drawing of Long Island is dwarfed by an enormous drawing of Manhattan.)

"If times get tough, will the city banks get going? (Back to the city.)

Fifteen months later, the same research was repeated. Notice how Long Island Trust's position improved in every attribute.

Many branches

Bank	Score
Long Island Trust	7.0
National Bank of North America	6.8
Chemical	6.6
Citibank	6.5
Chase Manhattan	6.1
European American	6.1

From last to first place in "many branches." In spite of the fact that Chemical Bank, for example, has more than twice as many branches on Long Island.

Full range of services

Bank	Score
Citibank	7.8
Chemical	7.8
Chase Manhattan	7.6
Long Island Trust	7.3
National Bank of North America	7.3
European American	7.2

In "full range of services" Long Island Trust moved up two spots. From sixth to fourth place.

The third advertisement in the Long Island Trust series. At the time of this campaign, New York City was having severe financial troubles. The Implication of the ad is that perhaps the city might want to dip into your account in order to balance its budget.

Quality of service	
Citibank	7.8
Chemical	7.6
Chase Manhattan	7.5
Long Island Trust	7.1
National Bank of North America	7.1
European American	7.0

In "quality of service" Long Island Trust also moved from sixth to fourth place.

Large capital	
Long Island Trust	7.0
Chemical	6.7
Citibank	6.7
National Bank of North America	6.6
Chase Manhattan	6.6
European American	6.4

In "large capital" Long Island Trust moved from last to first place.

Results were seen not only in the research but in the branches too. "With the assistance of the advertising agency which pioneered the widely accepted concept of positioning," said the bank's annual report, "our lead bank, Long Island Trust, assumed the mantle of the Long Island Bank for Long Islanders. Acceptance of the campaign was immediate and gratifying."

You might think that a bank promoting the area that it serves is an obvious idea. And it is.

Long Island Trust is no longer with us having been absorbed by a larger bank. Hopefully, the advertising enhanced their selling price.

But the best positioning ideas are so simple that most people overlook them.

19 Positioning the Catholic Church

This book could have been written about religion just as well as about advertising.

A far-fetched idea?

Not really. The essence of any religion is communication. From divinity to clergy to congregation.

The problems arise not with a perfect divinity or an imperfect congregation but with the clergy.

How the clergy applies communication theory to the practice of religion will have a major influence on the way religion affects the congregation.

An Identity Crisis

Not too long ago, positioning thinking was applied to the Catholic Church. In other words, communication problems of this enormous institution were treated as if they belonged to a major corporation.

This request did not come from the Pope or a committee of bishops. It came from a group of laity who were deeply concerned about what one renowned theologian dubbed a "certain crisis of identity" that had followed in the wake of the reforms of Vatican II.

It was quickly apparent that communication in the Catholic Church was haphazard at best.

While much effort had been expended in improving techniques, the programs lacked a strong central theme or any continuity. (An especially serious problem in an era of electronic overcommunication.)

It was like General Motors with no overall corporate advertising programs. All communication came from the local dealers. Some of it good, much of it bad.

A large measure of the problems could be traced to Vatican II.

Prior to that "opening of the windows," the institutional Church had a clearly perceived position in the minds of the faithful. To most, the Church was the teacher of the law. Much emphasis was placed on rules, rewards and punishment. The Church was consistent in its approach to old and young alike.

Vatican II moved the Catholic Church away from this posture of law and order. Many rules and regulations were dismissed as unnecessary. Changes in liturgy and style became commonplace. Flexibility took the place of rigidity.

Unfortunately, there was no advertising manager in Rome when these momentous changes were being made. No one to distill what had transpired and produce a program in simple language that explained the new directions.

After years of not needing a "corporate" communication program, it's understandable that the Catholic

Church failed to recognize the scope of the problem on its hands.

Losing Its Influence

What was painfully lacking was a clear presentation of what the new church was about.

The faithful quietly asked, "If you are not the teacher of the law, what are you?"

In the years since Vatican II, there has been no simple answer forthcoming. No attempt to reposition the church in the minds of the laity. Even in the minds of the clergy, for that matter.

And with no answers, confusion walked in and many people walked out.

For the first time, regular Mass attendance dropped below 50 percent of the Catholic population.

There are 20 percent fewer priests, nuns and brothers today than there were ten years ago. Vocations have dropped by 60 percent.

One final set of statistics is especially significant. The Catholic Church is presently the "largest community of moral authority in American society." (A title bestowed upon it recently by the Protestant theologian Peter Berger.)

Yet when a group of 24,000 highly influential executives were asked by *U.S. News & World Report* to rate the influence of major institutions, the Church and other organized religions came in dead last. (See table on next page.)

The moral authority of the Catholic Church was obviously not being communicated very well.

Labor unions	66 percent
Television	65 percent
Supreme Court	65 percent
White House	54 percent
Newspapers	47 percent
Government bureaucracy	46 percent
U.S. Senate	43 percent
U.S. House	36 percent
Industry	33 percent
Financial institutions	25 percent
Democratic Party	22 percent
Magazines	20 percent
Educational institutions	18 percent
The Cabinet	18 percent
Radio	15 percent
Advertising agencies	15 percent
Republican Party	8 percent
Organized religion	5 percent

What Role for the Church?

"What is the role of the Catholic Church in the modern world?"

This question was asked of clergy, bishops, laity. Never was the same answer received twice.

Some say there is no simple answer. Some say there's more than one answer. (Recognize the everybody trap.)

Corporate executives usually have answers to questions like this. If you ask the top executives at General Motors, they will more than likely see their role as being the world's largest manufacturer of automobiles. Companies spend millions finding and communicating the essence of their products with words like "Whiter than white" or "Fighting cavities is what Crest is all about."

The Church had to answer this unanswered question in simple, definitive terms. And it had to put this answer into a totally integrated communication program. Then it had to take this program to the flock in a new and dramatic way.

Working out an identity program for a corporation usually entails a retracing of steps until you discover the basic business of a company. This requires poring over old plans and programs. Seeing what worked and what didn't.

In the case of the Catholic Church, you have to go back 2,000 years and retrace the steps of the Church. Instead of old annual reports, you have to rely on Scripture.

In the search for a simple, direct expression of the role of the Church, two explicit statements in the Gospel could hold the answer.

First, during Christ's ministry on earth God, as reported in Matthew's Gospel, instructed man to listen to the words of his Son, the Beloved (Matt. 17:23).

Then Christ, as he departed from earth, instructed his followers to go and teach all nations what they had heard from him (Matt. 28:19).

Teacher of the Word

It's apparent from the Scriptures that Christ saw the role of the Church as "teacher of the word."

Because he was "the Son of God," it must be assumed that his word is a word for all ages. Christ's parables were not just for the people of his time, but also for now.

Hence they must have in their construction a universality which would never become dated. They are simple and deep. In them Jesus gives to people of all ages food for thought and action.

So it can be assumed that those who proclaim the message today can and should transmit the old message in a new form in their own locality, in their own time, in their own way.

Thus the retracing of steps led to defining the role of the Church as that of keeping Christ alive in the minds of each new generation and relating his word to the problems of their time.

In many ways Vatican II seemed to point the Church backwards rather than forward. From "teacher of the law" to "teacher of the word."

This may seem like a very simplistic, almost obvious answer to a complicated problem.

And it is. Experience has shown that a positioning exercise is a search for the obvious. Those are the easiest concepts to communicate because they make the most sense to the recipient of a message.

Unfortunately, obvious concepts are also the most difficult to recognize and to sell.

The human mind tends to admire the complicated and dismiss the obvious as being too simplistic. (For example, many clerics in the Catholic Church admire the definition of the role of the Church put forth by a noted theologian named Avery Dulles. His answer:

The Church hasn't one role. It has six different roles to play.)

Implementing the Position

Once the obvious concept had been isolated, the next thing to be done was to develop the techniques for implementing it.

First and foremost was pulpit training. To fulfill the role of "teacher of the word," the clergy had to become far better speakers and to give far better sermons. (Your best religious speakers today can be found not in church but on Sunday morning television).

In addition to pulpit training, an introductory film entitled *Return to the Beginning* was proposed.

The start of any major communication effort often needs some drama to get people's attention. The emotion of the film medium is ideal for this kind of effort. (Which is also why television is so powerful a tool for new product introductions.)

A wide range of other program elements was suggested, all carefully constructed around the role of the church as "teacher of the word."

The point here is that once a positioning strategy has been developed, it sets the direction for all the activities of the organization. Even one as large and multifaceted as the Catholic Church.

What Happened?

Nothing.

It has been very difficult to convince the management of the Catholic Church to implement this solution to their problems.

The current Pope took the Church back to its conservative past. We'll shortly see where the next one will head.

Not only do bishops resist having lay people tell them how to run their Church, but the solution appears to be much too obvious for them to accept. Simplicity is not as attractive as complexity.

But that's another book someday.

20 Positioning Yourself and Your Career

If positioning strategies can be used to promote a product, why can't they be used to promote yourself?

No reason at all.

So let's review positioning theory as it might apply to your own personal career.

Define Yourself

What are you? People suffer from the same disease as products. They try to be all things to all people.

The problem with this approach is the mind of the prospect. It's difficult enough to link one concept with each product. It's almost impossible with two or three or more concepts.

The most difficult part of positioning is selecting that one specific concept to hang your hat on. Yet you must, if you want to cut through the prospect's wall of indifference.

What are you? What is your own position in life? Can you sum up your own position in a single concept? Then can you run your own career to establish and exploit that position?

Most people aren't ruthless enough to set up a single concept for themselves. They vacillate. They expect others to do it for them.

"I'm the best lawyer in Dallas."

Are you? How often would your name be mentioned if we took a survey of the Dallas legal community?

"I'm the best lawyer in Dallas" is a position that can be achieved with some talent, some luck and a lot of strategy. And the first step is to isolate the concept that you are going to use to establish that long-term position. It's not easy. But the rewards can be great.

Make Mistakes

Anything worthwhile doing is worthwhile doing lousy. If it wasn't worthwhile doing, you shouldn't have done it at all.

On the other hand, if it is worthwhile doing and you wait until you can do it perfectly, if you procrastinate, you run the risk of not doing it. Ever.

Therefore, anything worthwhile doing is worthwhile doing lousy.

Your reputation will probably be better within the company if you try many times and succeed sometimes than if you fear failure and only try for sure things.

People still remember Ty Cobb, who stole 96 bases out of 134 tries (70 percent). But they have forgotton Max Carey, who stole 51 bases out of 53 (96 percent).

Eddie Arcaro, perhaps the greatest jockey who ever

rode a horse, had 250 straight losers before he rode his first winner.

Make Sure Your Name Is Right

Remember Leonard Slye? Few people did, until he changed his name to Roy Rogers, an important first step in becoming a motion picture star.

How about Marion Morrison? A little feminine for a he-man cowboy, so he changed it to John Wayne.

Or Issur Danielovitch? First changed to Isadore Demsky and then to Kirk Douglas.

"Fate tried to conceal him," said Oliver Wendell Holmes, Jr., "by naming him Smith."

Common law grants you the right to adopt any name you want as long as you're not trying to defraud or be deceptive. So don't change your name to McDonald and open up a hamburger stand.

Also, if you're a politician, don't bother to change your name to "None of the Above." Luther D. Knox, a candidate in a Louisiana gubernatorial primary, had his name legally changed to just that. However, a federal judge had Mr. None of the Above's name taken off the ballot because the move was deceptive.

What would you do if your name was Ralph Lifshitz? Would you change your name to Ralph Lauren as Ralph Lifshitz did? Don't be too sure. Over the years we have suggested to many business people that they change their own names. So far no one has taken our advice.

Avoid the No-Name Trap

Many business people fall victim to initialitus personally as well as corporately.

As young executives, they notice that top managers usually use initials: J. S. Smith, R. H. Jones. So they do the same. On memos and in letters.

It's a mistake. You can afford to do that only if everyone knows who you are. If you're on your way up, if you're trying to burn your name into the minds of top managment, you need a name, not a set of initials. For exactly the same reasons your company does.

Write your name out and look at it. Roger P. Dinkelacker.

What a name like this says psychologically to managment is: We are such a big company and you have such an insignificant job that you must use the "P" to differentiate yourself from the other Roger Dinkelackers on the staff.

Not likely.

It is possible, if your name is something like John Smith or Mary Jones, that you actually do need a middle initial to differentiate yourself from the other John Smiths or Mary Joneses.

If so, what you really need is a new name. Confusion is the enemy of successful positioning. You can't "burn in" a name that's too common. How are other people going to differentiate between John T. Smith and John S. Smith?

They won't bother. They'll just forget you along with the rest. And the no-name trap will have claimed another victim.

Avoid the Line-Extension Trap

If you had three daughters, would you name them Mary 1, Mary 2 and Mary 3? As a matter of fact, would you name them Mary, Marian and Marilyn? Either way, you're creating a lifetime of confusion.

When you hang a junior on your son's name, you do him no favor. He deserves a separate identity.

In show business, where you must burn a clear-cut identity in the mind of the public, even a famous last name should probably not be used.

Today Liza Minnelli is a bigger star than her mother, Judy Garland, ever was. As Liza Garland, she would have started with a handicap.

Frank Sinatra, Jr., is an example of the most difficult kind of line-extension name. He literally started with two strikes against him.

With a name like Frank Sinatra, Jr., the audience says to itself, "He's not going to be able to sing as well as his father."

Since you hear what you expect to hear, of course he doesn't.

Nor for that matter did Will Rogers, Jr., make much of a name for himself.

This issue deserves much more comment. When both parent and child are on the scene at the same time, the "Junior" designation is usually the kiss of death. (Frank Sinatra and Frank Sinatra, Jr.) On the other hand, people brands can be transferred from one generation to the next and in the process become extremely powerful. This is especially true in politics. Witness the power of people brands like Roosevelt, Kennedy, Bush, and Gore.

Find a Horse to Ride

Some ambitious, intelligent people find themselves trapped in situations where their future looks bleak. So what do they generally do?

They try harder. They try to compensate by long hours of hard work and effort. The secret of success is to keep your nose to the grindstone, do your job better than the next person, and fame and fortune will come your way, right?

Wrong. Trying harder is rarely the pathway to success. Trying smarter is the better way.

It's the story of the shoemaker's children all over again. Too often, management people don't know how to manage their own careers.

Their own promotional strategy is often based on the naive assumption that ability and hard work are all that counts. And so they dig in and work harder, waiting for the day that someone will tap them on the shoulder with the magic wand.

But that day seldom comes.

The truth is, the road to fame and fortune is rarely found within yourself. The only sure way to success is to find yourself a horse to ride. It may be difficult for the ego to accept, but success in life is based more on what others can do for you than on what you can do for yourself.

Kennedy was wrong. Ask not what you can do for your company. Ask what your company can do for you. Therefore, if you want to take maximum advantage of the opportunities that your career has to offer, you must keep your eyes open and find yourself a horse to do the job for you.

1. The First Horse to Ride Is Your Company. Where is your company going? Or more impolitely, is it going anywhere at all?

Too many good people have taken their good prospects and locked them into situations that are doomed to failure. But failure at least gives you a second chance. Even worse is the company with less than average chances for growth.

No matter how brilliant you are, it never pays to

cast your lot with a loser. Even the best officer on the Titantic wound up in the same lifeboat as the worst. And that's if he was lucky enough to stay out of the water.

You can't do it yourself. If your company is going nowhere, get yourself a new one. While you can't always pick an IBM or a Xerox, you ought to be able to do considerably better than average.

Place your bets on the growth industries. Tomorrow-type products like computers, electronics, optics, communications.

And don't forget that soft services of all types are growing at a much faster rate than hard products. So look at banks, leasing, insurance, medical, financial and consulting service companies.

Don't forget that your experience with yesterday-type products can blind you to opportunities in totally different product areas. And especially services.

And when you change jobs to join one of those tomorrow-type companies, don't just ask how much they are going to pay you today.

Also ask how much they are likely to pay you tomorrow.

2. The Second Horse to Ride Is Your Boss. Ask yourself the same questions about your boss as you asked yourself about your company.

Is he or she going anywhere? If not, who is? Always try to work for the smartest, brightest, most competent person you can find.

If you look at biographies of successful people, it's amazing to find how many crawled up the ladder of success right behind someone else. From their first

Microsoft
Intel
Cisco
Yahoo!
Oracle
Dell
Starbucks
Wal-Mart
Home Depot

If you had cast your lot early on with almost any of these companies, you couldn't help but be rich today.

assignment in some menial job to their last as president or CEO of a major company.

Yet some people actually like to work for incompetents. I suppose they feel that a fresh flower stands out better if it's surrounded by wilted ones. They forget the tendency of top management to throw the whole bunch out if they become dissatisfied with an operation

Two types of individuals come in looking for jobs

One is inordinately proud of his or her specialty. He or she will often say, "You people really need me around here. You're weak in my specialty."

The other type says just the opposite. "You're strong in my specialty. You do a terrific job, and I want to work with the best."

Which type is more likely to get the job? Right. The latter person.

On the other hand, strange as it might seem, top management people see more of the other type. The person who wants to be an expert. Preferably with a big title and salary to match.

"Hitch your wagon to a star," said Ralph Waldo Emerson. Good advice then. Even better advice now.

If your boss is going places, chances are good that you are too.

3. The Third Horse to Ride Is a Friend. Many business people have an enormous number of personal friends but no business friends. And while personal friends are awfully nice to have and can sometimes get you a deal on a TV set or braces for the kids, they're usually not too helpful when it comes to finding a better job.

Most of the big breaks that happen in a person's

career happen because a business friend recommended that person.

The more business friends you make outside of your own organization, the more likely you are to wind up in a big, rewarding job.

It's not enough just to make friends. You have to take out that friendship horse and exercise it once in a while. If you don't, you won't be able to ride it when you need it.

When an old business friend you haven't heard from in ten years calls you and wants to have lunch, you know two things will happen: (1) you're going to pay for the lunch, and (2) your friend is looking for a job.

When you need a job, it's usually too late to try that type of tactic. The way to ride the friendship horse is to keep in touch regularly with all your business friends.

Send them tear sheets of articles they may be interested in, clips of publicity items and congratulatory letters when they get promoted.

And don't assume people always see stories that might have mentioned them. They don't. And they always appreciate it when someone sends them an item they may have missed.

4. The Fourth Horse to Ride Is an Idea. On the night before he died, Victor Hugo wrote in his diary, "Nothing, not all the armies of the world, can stop an idea whose time has come."

Everyone knows that an idea can take you to the top faster than anything else. But people sometimes expect too much of an idea. They want one that is not only great, but one that everyone else thinks is great too.

There are no such ideas. If you wait until an idea is ready to be accepted, it's too late. Someone else will have preempted it.

Or in the in-out vocabulary of a few years ago: Anything definitely in is already on its way out.

To ride the "idea" horse, you must be willing to expose yourself to ridicule and controversy. You must be willing to go against the tide.

You can't be first with a new idea or concept unless you are willing to stick your neck out. And take a lot of abuse.

And bide your time until your time comes.

So, too, with the positioning concept. The controversy was a factor in keeping the idea alive and talked about.

It wasn't long after the positioning articles appeared in *Advertising Age* that Leo Greenland wrote an article condemning the authors. "Gurus and cultists" were two of the nicer things he had to say.

Even the head of the most respected advertising agency in the world summed up our positioning concept with one word.

"Nonsense," said Bill Bernbach at an Association of National Advertisers meeting at the Homestead.

"One indication of the validity of a principle," according to psychologist Charles Osgood, "is the vigor and persistence with which it is opposed. In any field," says Dr. Osgood, "if people see that a principle is obvious nonsense and easy to refute, they tend to ignore it. On the other hand, if the principle is difficult to refute and it causes them to question some of their own basic assumptions with which their names may be identified, they have to go out of their way to find something wrong with it."

Never be afraid of conflict.

Where would Winston Churchill have been without Adolf Hitler? We know the answer to that one. After Adolf Hitler was disposed of, at the very first opportunity the British public promptly turned Winston Churchill out of office.

And you remember what Liberace said about the bad reviews one of his concerts received. "I cried all the way to the bank."

An idea or concept without an element of conflict is not an idea at all. It's motherhood, apple pie and the flag, revisited.

5. The Fifth Horse to Ride Is Faith. Faith in others and their ideas. The importance of getting outside of yourself, of finding your fortune on the outside, is illustrated by the story of a man who was a failure most of his life.

His name was Ray Kroc, and he was a lot older than most people and a failure to boot when he met two brothers who changed his life.

For the brothers had an idea, but no faith. So they sold their idea as well as their name to Ray Kroc for relatively few dollars.

Today Ray Kroc may be the richest man in America. Worth hundreds of millions of dollars.

The brothers? They were the McDonald brothers, and every time you eat one of their hamburgers, remember it was the vision, courage and persistence of

In 1989, we expanded this chapter into a book called *Horse Sense*, which did poorly in the marketplace, Lesson learned: We have no credentials in the self-motivation business. Leave that to Tony Robbins and Tom Peters.

the outsider who made the McDonald's chain a success.

Not two guys named McDonald.

6. The Sixth Horse to Ride Is Yourself. There is one other horse. An animal that is mean, difficult and unpredictable. Yet people often try to ride it. With very little success.

That horse is yourself. It is possible to succeed in business or in life all by yourself. But it's not easy.

Like life itself, business is a social activity. As much cooperation as competition.

Take selling, for example. You don't make a sale all by yourself. Somebody has to buy.

So remember, the winningest jockeys are not necessarily the lightest, the smartest or the strongest. The best jockey doesn't win the race.

The jockey that wins the race is usually the one with the best horse.

So pick yourself a horse to ride and then ride it for all it's worth.

21 Six Steps to Success

How do you get started on a positioning program?

It's not easy. The temptation is to work on the solution without first thinking through the problem. Much better to think about your situation in an organized way before leaping to a conclusion.

To help you with this thinking process, here are six questions you can ask yourself to get your mental juices flowing.

Don't be deceived. The questions are simple to ask but difficult to answer. They often raise soul-searching issues that can test your courage and your beliefs.

1. What Position Do You Own?

Positioning is thinking in reverse. Instead of starting with yourself, you start with the mind of the prospect.

Instead of asking what you are, you ask what position you already own in the mind of the prospect.

Changing minds in our overcommunicated society is an extremely difficult task. It's much easier to work with what's already there.

In determining the state of the prospect's mind, it's important not to let corporate egos get in the way. You get the answer to the question "What position do we own?" from the marketplace, not from the marketing manager.

If this requires a few dollars for research, so be it. Spend the money. It's better to know exactly what you're up against now than to discover it later when nothing can be done about it.

Don't be narrow-minded. You must look at the big picture, not the details.

Sabena's problem is not Sabena, the airline, but Belgium, the country.

Seven-Up's problem is not the prospect's attitude toward lemon/lime drinks, but the overwhelming share of mind occupied by the colas. "Get me a soda," to many people, means a Coke or a Pepsi.

Looking at the big picture helped Seven-Up develop its successful uncola program.

Most products today are like 7-Up before the uncola campaign. They have weak or nonexistent positions in the minds of most prospects.

What you must do is to find a way into the mind by hooking your product, service or concept to what's already there.

2. What Position Do You Want to Own?

Here is where you bring out your crystal ball and try to figure out the best position to own from a long-term point of view. "Own" is the key word. Too many programs set out to communicate a position that is impossible to preempt because someone else already owns it.

Ford failed to position the Edsel successfully. One reason was there simply was no room in the mind of the auto buyer for another heavily chromed, medium-priced car.

On the other hand, when Richardson Merrill was trying to position an entry in the cold-remedy field against Contac and Dristan, it wisely avoided a direct confrontation. Leaving these two to fight it out in the daylight hours, Richardson Merrill chose to preempt the "nighttime cold remedy" position for Nyquil.

Nyquil turned out to be the most successful new product they have introduced in recent years.

Sometimes you can want too much. You can want to own a position that's too broad. A position that can't be established in the prospect's mind. And even if it could, it couldn't be defended against the assaults of narrowly based products like Nyquil.

This, of course, is the everybody trap, and one example is a famous campaign for a beer called Rheingold. This brewery wanted to preempt New York City's working class. (Not a bad objective when you consider the large number of heavy beer drinkers in this group.)

So they produced some marvelous commercials featuring Italians drinking Rheingold, Blacks drinking Rheingold, Irisn drinking Rheingold, Jews drinking Rheingold, and so on.

Well, rather than appeal to everybody, they ended

up appealing to nobody. The reason was simple. Prejudice being a basic human commodity, the fact that one ethnic group drank Rheingold sure didn't impress another ethnic group.

In fact, all the campaign did was alienate every ethnic group in New York.

While Rheingold faltered, the F&M Schaefer Brewing Company successfully positioned Schaefer for New York's heavy beer drinker with their famous "The one beer to have when you're having more than one" slogan. They recognized that the "heavy user" position was available and moved to preempt it.

In your own career, it's easy to make the same mistake. If you try to be all things to all people, you wind up with nothing. Better to narrow the focus of your expertise. To establish a unique position as a specialist, not as a jack-of-all-trades generalist.

The job market today belongs to the people who can define and position themselves as specialists.

3. Whom Must You Outgun?

If your proposed position calls for a head-to-head approach against a marketing leader, forget it. It's better to go around an obstacle rather than over it. Back up. Try to select a position that no one else has a firm grip on.

You must spend as much time thinking about the situation from the point of view of your competitors as you do thinking about it from your own.

Football is an easy game to play if you look at it from your own point of view. To rack up six points,

all you have to do is carry the ball across the goal line.

What makes football difficult is not the problem of scoring. (The problem of defining a position, if you will.) What makes football difficult is the 11 men in between you and the goal line. (The problem of establishing the position.)

Coming to grips with the competition is also the main problem in most marketing situations.

4. Do You Have Enough Money?

A big obstacle to successful positioning is attempting to achieve the impossible. It takes money to build a share of mind. It takes money to establish a position. It takes money to hold a position once you've established it.

The noise level today is fierce. There are just too many me-too products and too many me-too companies vying for the mind of the prospect. Getting noticed is getting tougher.

During the course of a single year, the average human mind is exposed to some 200,000 advertising messages. When you remember that a 30-second $243,000 Super Bowl commercial can make only one of those 200,000 impressions, the odds against an advertiser today must be seen as enormous.

This is why a company like Procter & Gamble is such a formidable competitor. When it bets on a new product, it will slide $20 million on the table, look around at the competition, and say, "Your bet."

If you don't spend enough to get above the noise level, you allow the Procter & Gambles of this world to take your concept away from you. One way to cope with the noise-level problem is to reduce the geographical scope of your problem. To introduce new products or new ideas on a market-by-market basis rather than nationally or even internationally.

With a given number of dollars, it's better to overspend in one city than to underspend in several cities. If you become successful in one location, you can always roll out the program to other places. Provided the first location is appropriate.

If you can become the No. 1 scotch in New York (the No. 1 scotch-drinking area of the country), you can roll out the product to the rest of the U.S.A.

5. Can You Stick It Out?

You can think of our overcommunicated society as a constant crucible of change. As one idea replaces another in bewildering succession.

To cope with change, it's important to take a long-range point of view. To determine your basic position and then stick to it.

Positioning is a concept that is cumulative. Something that takes advantage of advertising's long-range nature.

You have to hang in there, year after year. Most successful companies rarely change a winning formula. How many years have you seen those Marlboro men riding into the sunset? Crest has been fighting cavities for so long they're into their second generation of kids. Because of change, a company must think even more strategically than it did before.

With rare exceptions, a company should almost never change its basic positioning strategy. Only its tactics, those short-term maneuvers that are intended to implement a long-term strategy.

The trick is to take that basic strategy and improve it. Find new ways to dramatize it. New ways to avoid the boredom factor. In other words, new ways to have Ronald McDonald end up eating a hamburger.

Owning a position in the mind is like owning a valuable piece of real estate. Once you give it up, you might find it's impossible to get it back again.

The line-extension trap is a good example. What you are really doing when you line-extend is weakening your basic position. And once that's gone, you are adrift without an anchor.

Levi's line-extended into casual clothes. And then found its basic position in jeans undermined by "designer label" jeans.

6. Do You Match Your Position?

Creative people often resist positioning thinking because they believe it restricts their creativity.

And you know what? It does. Positioning thinking does restrict creativity.

One of the great communication tragedies is to watch an organization go through a careful planning exercise, step by step, complete with charts and graphs and then turn the strategy over to the "creatives" for execution. They, in turn, apply their skills and the strategy disappears in a cloud of technique, never to be recognized again

An institution like this would have been much better off running the flip-chart with the strategy on it rather than the ad with thousands of dollars worth of creativity applied.

"Avis is only No. 2 in rent-a-cars, so why go with us? We try harder." This doesn't sound like an ad. It sounds like the presentation of the marketing strategy. In truth, it's both.

Do your advertisements for yourself match your position? Do your clothes, for example, tell the world that you're a banker or a lawyer or an artist?

Or do you wear creative clothes that undermine your position?

Creativity by itself is worthless. Only when it is subordinated to the positioning objective can creativity make a contribution.

The Role of the Outsider

The question sometimes arises: Do we do it ourselves or do we hire someone to position us?

The someone that often gets hired is an advertising agency. An ad agency? Who needs help from those Madison Avenue hucksters?

Everybody. But only the rich can afford to hire an advertising agency. All the others have to learn how to do it themselves. Have to learn how to apply the invaluable ingredient only available from the outsider.

And what does the outsider supply? An ingredient called ignorance. In other words, objectivity.

By not knowing what goes on inside a company,

the outsider is better able to see what is happening on the outside. In the mind of the prospect.

The outsider is naturally attuned to outside-in thinking, while the insider is more comfortable with inside-out thinking. (No wonder clients sometimes have trouble getting along with their agencies.)

Objectivity is the key ingredient supplied by the advertising or marketing communication or public relations agency.

What the Outsider Doesn't Supply

In a word, magic. Some business managers believe that the role of an advertising agency is to wave a magic wand which causes prospects to immediately rush out and buy the product.

The wand, of course, is called "creativity," a commodity much sought after by the neophyte advertiser.

The popular view is that the agency "creates." And that the best agencies are filled with a substance called "creativity" which they liberally apply to their advertising solutions.

In advertising circles, the story is told about an advertising agency that was very creative. So creative, in fact, it could take straw and spin it into gold.

Now you might have heard of them because they had a very creative name. Rumplestiltskin, Inc.

The legend lives on. Even today, some people think agencies are so creative that they can spin straw into gold.

Not true. Advertising agencies can't spin straw

We were wrong. Creativity is not dead; It's still running rampant up and down Madison Avenue. While everyone uses the word "positioning," we're not too sure that many advertising people know what the word really means.

into gold. If they could, they'd be in the straw-spinning business and not the advertising business.

Today, creativity is dead. The name of the game on Madison Avenue is positioning.

22 Playing the Positioning Game

Some people have trouble playing the positioning game because they are hung up on words.

They assume, incorrectly, that words have meanings. They let Mr. Webster rule their life.

You Must Understand Words

As general semanticists have been saying for decades, words don't contain meanings. The meanings are not in the words. They are in the people using the words.

Like a sugar bowl which is empty until someone fills it with sugar, a word has no meaning until someone uses it and fills it with meaning.

If you try to add sugar to a leaky sugar bowl, you won't get anywhere. So, too, if you try to add meaning to a leaky word. Much better to discard that leaky word and use another.

The word "Volkswagen" won't hold the concept of a medium-sized luxury car, so you discard that sugar bowl and use another, "Audi," which holds the concept better. You don't insist that because it's made in a Volkswagen factory, it must be a Volkswagen. Mental rigidity is a barrier to successful positioning.

To be successful today at positioning, you must have a large degree of mental flexibility. You must be able to select and use words with as much disdain for the history book as for the dictionary.

Not that conventional, accepted meanings are not important. Quite the contrary. You must select the words which trigger the meanings you want to establish.

How would you position a country like Poland?

Too many Polish jokes have polluted the sugar bowl named Poland. So you first change the name of that beautiful country on the Vistula and Oder rivers. The land of Warsaw and Szczecin.

But is this ethical? After all, the country *is* Poland.

Is it? Remember, words have no meaning. They are empty containers until you fill them with meaning. If you want to reposition a product, a person or a country, you often have to first change the container.

In a sense, every product or service is "packaged goods." If it isn't sold in a box, the name becomes the box.

You Must Understand People

Words are triggers. They trigger the meanings which are buried in the mind.

Of course, if people understood this, there would be no advantage in renaming a product or selecting emotional words like Mustang for an automobile.

But they don't. Most people are unsane. They're not completely sane and they're not completely insane. They're somewhere in between.

What's the difference between sane people and insane people? What exactly do insane people do? Alfred Korzybski, who developed the concept of general semantics, explains that insane people try to make the world of reality fit what is in their heads.

The insane person who thinks he is Napoleon makes the outside world fit that notion.

The sane person constantly analyzes the world of reality and then changes what's inside his or her head to fit the facts.

That's an awful lot of trouble for most people. Besides, how many people want to constantly change their opinions to fit the facts?

It's a whole lot easier to change the facts to fit your opinions.

Unsane people make up their minds and then find the facts to "verify" the opinion. Or even more commonly, they accept the opinion of the nearest "expert," and then they don't have to bother with the facts at all. (Word of mouth.)

So you see the power of the psychologically right name. The mind makes the world of reality fit the name. A Mustang looks sportier, racier and faster than if the same car had been called the Turtle.

Language is the currency of the mind. To think conceptually, you manipulate words. With the right choice of words, you can influence the thinking process itself. (As proof that the mind "thinks with words" and not abstract thoughts, consider how a language is learned. To be really fluent in a foreign language, say French, you must learn to think in French.)

But there are limits. If a word is so far out of touch with reality, the mind just refuses to use the word. It says "large" on the tube that everyone except the manufacturer calls a "small tube of toothpaste." It says "economy" on the toothpaste tube that everyone calls "large."

The People's Republic of China is usually called "Red China" because no one believes it is a "people's republic." (Inside the country, the People's Republic of China is undoubtedly an effective name.)

You Must Be Careful of Change

The more things change, the more they remain the same. Yet people today are caught up in the illusion of change. Every day, the world seems to be turning faster.

Years ago a successful product might live 50 years or more before fading away. Today a product's life cycle is much shorter. Sometimes it can be measured in months instead of years.

New products, new services, new markets, even new media are constantly being born. They grow to adulthood and then slide to oblivion. And a new cycle starts again.

Yesterday the well-groomed man had his hair cut every week. Today it's every month or two.

Yesterday the way to reach the masses was the mass magazines. Today it's network TV. Tomorrow it could be cable. The only permanent thing today seems to be change. The kaleidoscope of life clicks faster and faster. New patterns emerge and disappear.

Change has become a way of life for many companies. But is change the way to keep pace with change? The exact opposite appears to be true.

The landscape is littered with the debris of projects that companies rushed into in attempting to keep pace. Singer trying to move into the boom in home appliances. RCA moving into the boom in computers. General Foods moving into the boom in fast-food outlets. Not to mention the hundreds of companies that threw away their corporate identities to chase the passing fad to initials.

Meanwhile the programs of those who kept at what they did best and held their ground have been immensely successful. Maytag selling its reliable appliances. Walt Disney selling his world of fantasy and fun. Avon calling.

And take margarine. Thirty years ago the first successful margarine brands positioned themselves against butter. "Tastes like the high-priced spread," said a typical ad. And what works today? Why the same strategy. "It isn't nice to fool Mother Nature," say the Chiffon commercials.

What do you need to play the positioning game successfully today?

You Need Vision

Change is a wave on the ocean of time. Short-term, the waves cause agitation and confusion. Long-term, the underlying currents are much more significant. To cope with change, you have to take a long-range point of view. To determine your basic business and stick with it.

Changing the direction of a large company is like trying to turn an aircraft carrier. It takes a mile before anything happens. And if it was a wrong turn, getting back on course takes even longer.

To play the game successfully, you must make decisions on what your company will be doing not next month or next year but in five years, ten years. In other words, instead of turning the wheel to meet each fresh wave, a company must point itself in the right direction.

You must have vision. There's no sense building a position based on a technology that's too narrow. Or a product that's becoming obsolete. Or a name that's defective.

Most of all, you have to be able to see the difference between what works and what doesn't work.

Sounds simple, but it's not. When the tide is rising, everything seems to be working. When the tide is falling, nothing seems to be working.

You have to learn how to separate your efforts from the general movement of the economy. Many marketing experts are blessed with a generous supply of luck. Be wary. Today's hula-hoop marketing genius could be tomorrow's welfare recipient.

Be patient. The sun shines tomorrow on those who have made the right decisions today.

If a company has positioned itself in the right direction, it will be able to ride the currents of change,

ready to take advantage of those opportunities that are right for it. But when an opportunity arrives, a company must move quickly.

You Need Courage

When you trace the history of how leadership positions were established, from Hershey in chocolate to Hertz in rent-a-cars, the common thread is not marketing skill or even product innovation. The common thread is seizing the initiative before the competitor has a chance to get established. In old-time military terms, the marketing leader "got there firstest with the mostest." The leader usually poured in the marketing money while the situation was still fluid.

Hershey, for example, established a position in chocolate so strong that Hershey felt it didn't need to advertise at all. This conviction was a luxury that competitors like Mars couldn't afford.

Finally Hershey decided to advertise. But not in time. Today the Hershey milk chocolate bar is not the largest seller. It's not even in the top five.

You can see that establishing a leadership position depends not only on luck and timing, but also upon a willingness to pour it on when others stand back and wait.

You Need Objectivity

To be successful in the positioning era, you must be brutally frank. You must try to eliminate all ego from the decision-making process. It only clouds the issue.

One of the most critical aspects of positioning is being able to evaluate products objectively and see how they are viewed by customers and prospects.

You also have to remember that you can't play basketball without a backboard. You need someone to bounce your ideas off. As soon as you think you have found that simple idea that is the solution to your problem, you have lost something.

You have lost your objectivity. You need the other person to take a fresh look at what you have wrought. And vice versa.

Like Ping-Pong, positioning is a game best played by two people. It's no accident that this book was written by two people. Only in a give-and-take atmosphere can ideas be refined and perfected.

You Need Simplicity

Only an obvious idea will work today. The overwhelming volume of communication prevents anything else from succeeding.

But the obvious isn't always so obvious. "Boss" Kettering had a sign which he placed on the wall of the General Motors Research Building in Dayton: "This problem when solved will be simple."

"Raisins from California. Nature's candy."

"Moist and meaty Gainesburgers. The canned dog food without the can."

"Bubble Yum. Number yum in bubble gum."

These are the kinds of simple ideas that work today. Simple concepts expressed with simple words used in a straightforward way.

Often the solution to a problem is so simple that thousands of people have looked at it without seeing it. When an idea is clever or complicated, however, we should be suspicious. It probably won't work because it's not simple enough.

The history of science is a history of the Ketterings of this world who found simple solutions to complex problems.

The head of an advertising agency once insisted that his account executives paste down the marketing strategy on the back of each layout.

Then when the client asked what the ad was supposed to do, the account person could turn the layout over and read the strategy.

But an ad should be simple enough so that it is the strategy.

The agency made a mistake. It ran the wrong side of the layout.

You Need Subtlety

Beginners who play the positioning game often remark, "How easy this is. You just find a position you can call your own."

Simple, yes. But easy, no.

The difficulty is finding an open position that's also effective.

In politics, for example, it's easy to establish a position to the far right (a conservative position) or the far left (a socialist position). You will undoubtedly preempt either position.

You will also lose.

What you must do is to find an opening near the center of the spectrum. You must be slightly conservative in a field of liberals or slightly liberal in a field of conservatives.

This calls for great restraint and subtlety. The big winners in business and in life are those people who have found open positions near the center of the spectrum. Not at the edge.

You can sometimes have a positioning success and a sales failure. This might be termed "Rolls-Royce thinking."

"We're the Rolls-Royce of the industry" is a claim you often hear in business today.

Do you know how many Rolls-Royces are sold every year?

Very few. Only a few thousand a year, compared to nearly half a million Cadillacs. (In the United Kingdom today, it's a shock to see Rolls-Royce ads in Arabic. But at $60,000 and up, mostly up, the market is very narrow.)

Both Cadillac and Rolls-Royce are luxury cars, but the gulf between them is enormous. To the average automobile buyer, the Rolls-Royce is out of reach.

Cadillac, like Michelob and other premium products, is not. The secret to establishing a successful position is to keep two things in balance: (1) a unique position with (2) broad appeal.

You Need Patience

Very few companies can afford to launch a new product on a nationwide scale.

Instead they look for places to make the brand successful. And then roll it out to other markets.

The geographic roll-out is one way. You build the product in one market and then move on to another. From east to west. Or vice versa.

The demographic roll-out is another. Philip Morris built Marlboro into the No. 1 cigarette on college campuses long before it became the No. 1 brand nationwide.

The chronologic roll-out is the third way. You build the brand among a specific age group and then roll it out to others. "The Pepsi Generation" was an effort by Pepsi-Cola to build the product among the younger set and then to reap the benefits as they grew up.

Distribution is another roll-out technique. The Wella line was first sold through beauty salons. After the products were established, they were sold through drugstores and supermarkets.

You Need a Global Outlook

Don't overlook the importance of worldwide thinking. A company that keeps its eye on Tom, Dick and Harry is going to miss Pierre, Hans and Yoshio.

Marketing is rapidly becoming a worldwide ballgame. A company that owns a position in one country now finds that it can use that position to wedge its way into another. IBM has some 60 percent of the German computer market. Is this fact surprising? It shouldn't be. IBM earns more than 50 percent of its profits outside the United States.

As companies start to operate on a worldwide basis, they often discover they have a name problem.

A typical example is U.S. Rubber, a worldwide company that marketed many products not made of rubber. Changing the name to Uniroyal created a new corporate identity that could be used worldwide.

You Need to Be "They"-Oriented

There are two kinds of marketing people. "We" people and "they" people.

"We" people have trouble understanding the essence of the new concept: You don't position the product in the sales manager's office. You position the product in the prospect's mind.

"We" people turn out in droves for self-help seminars. We people are convinced that with proper motivation, anything is possible.

"We" people make dynamic speakers. 'Our will, our determination, our hard work, our superior sales force, our loyal distributors, our this and our that. With these things, we will be successful."

Maybe. But "they" people usually see things more clearly. "They" people focus their attention on the competition. "They" people scan the marketplace like a general scans the battlefield. "They" people seek out competitive weaknesses to exploit and learn to avoid competitive strengths.

In particular, "they" people rapidly abandon the illusion that superior people are the key to success.

"We have the best people" is probably the biggest illusion of all. As every general knows deep in his

In 1988, we expanded the "we versus they" concept into a book called *Bottom-Up Marketing*. You don't find a position inside the company. You find your position on the outside in terms of a tactic that will work in the mind of the prospect. Then you bring the tactic back inside the company where you develop a strategy to exploit the tactic.

heart, the differences in fighting abilities of the individual soldiers in different armies are always very slight. One side or the other might have better training or superior equipment, but inherent ability evens out when large numbers of men are involved.

So it is with companies. If you believe that person for person your company is superior to your competitors, then you are likely to believe in anything. Santa Claus. The Tooth Fairy.

The leveling factor, of course, is the numbers. While it's possible to recruit one superior person out of a limited number of potential employees, it's another problem altogether to get ten. Or a hundred. Or a thousand.

The application of a little mathematics will tell you that any company that employs several hundred people or more can expect no difference in average quality of personnel over its competitors. (Unless, of course, it pays its people more. But that's sacrificing quantity for quality, which is not necessarily an advantage.)

When General Motors goes out in the field to do battle with Ford, you know that the outcome will not depend on the abilities of the individuals involved.

The outcome will depend on which side has the better generals and hence the better strategy. With the advantage on the side of General Motors, to be sure.

What You Don't Need

You don't need a reputation as a marketing genius. As a matter of fact, this could be a fatal flaw.

All too often, the product leader makes the fatal mistake of attributing its success to marketing skill. As a result, it thinks it can transfer that skill to other products and other marketing situations.

Witness, for example, the sorry record of Xerox in computers.

And the mecca of marketing knowledge, International Business Machines Corporation, hasn't done much better. So far, IBM's plain-paper copier hasn't made much of a dent in Xerox's business. Touché.

"Don't go head to head with an established leader" became a mantra with us. In 1985, we expanded this concept into a book called *Marketing Warfare* which is still a big seller today.

The rules of positioning hold for all types of products. In the packaged goods area, for example, Bristol-Myers tried to take on Crest toothpaste with Fact (killed after $5 million was spent on promotion). Then they tried to go after Alka-Seltzer with Resolve (killed after $11 million was spent). Then they tried to unseat Bayer with Dissolve, another financial headache. And then came the attack on Tylenol with Datril. An even worse headache.

The suicidal bent of companies that go head-on against established competition is hard to understand. They know the score, yet they forge ahead anyway. In the marketing war, a "charge of the light brigade" happens every day.

With the same predictable result.

Most companies are in the No. 2, 3, 4 or even worse category. What then?

Hope springs eternal in the human breast. Nine times out of ten, the also-ran sets out to attack the leader, like RCA's assault on IBM. Result: Disaster

To repeat, the first rule of positioning is: To win the battle for the mind, you can't compete head-on against a company that has a strong, established position. You can go around, under or over, but never head-to-head.

The leader owns the high ground. The No. 1 position in the prospect's mind. The top rung of the product ladder. To move up the ladder, you must follow the rules of positioning.

In our overcommunicated society, the name of the game today is positioning.

And only the better players are going to survive.

The law of leadership is obviously the first and most important law of marketing. But what do you do if you're not the leader? In 1993, we answered that question (and many others) in the book, *The 22 Immutable Laws of Marketing.* Key observation: If you're not the leader, set up a new category you can be the leader in.

Over the years, we've also written countless articles that focus on different aspects of this 20-year-old book. If nothing else, we have been consistent in our beliefs. It's just that we continue to come across people who don't believe us. One who did was Harvard's Michael Porter. He used "Positioning" for his competitive advantage.

Index

About the Authors

Al Ries is Chairman of Ries & Ries, Roswell, Georgia.

Jack Trout is President of Trout & Partners, Old Greenwich, Connecticut.

Al Ries and Jack Trout are undoubtedly the world's best-known marketing strategists.